THERE AND BACK

CHRIS NICHOLSON

¤

THERE AND BACK

SWIFTNICK
2005

First published in 2001 by
Swiftnick
60 New Street
Halstead
Essex CO9 1DD

A catalogue record for this book is available from the British Library.

ISBN 1-84363-000-1

Reprinted 2002, 2004, 2005

Typeset in New Century 11/12pt
by Scriptmate Editions from the author's disk

Manufacture co-ordinated in UK by Book-in-Hand Ltd
20 Shepherds Hill, London N6 5AH

Contents

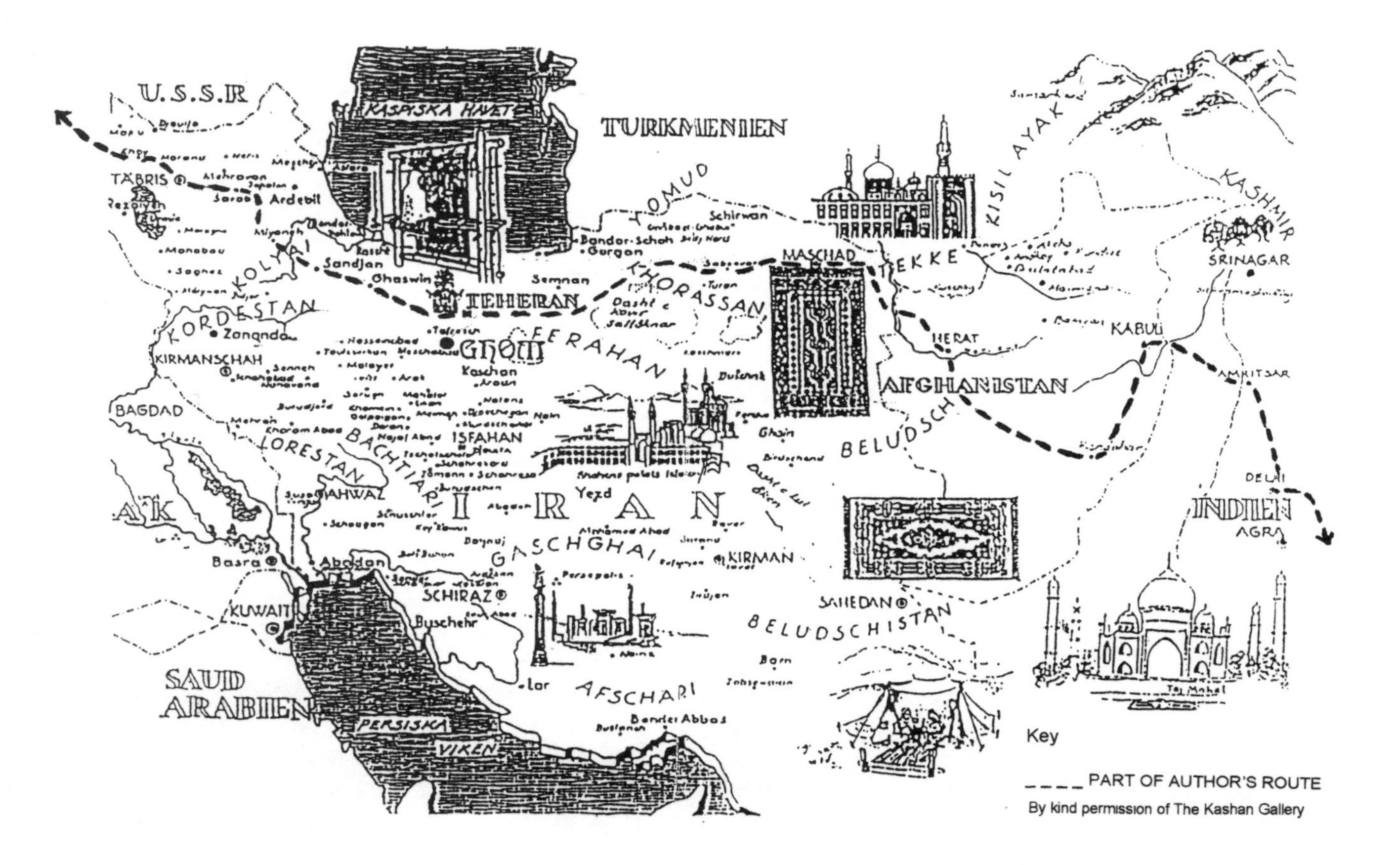

By kind permission of The Kashan Gallery

THERE

I. TO THE RUBICON

IT WAS THE LAST DAY of cricket in England that summer being shown on the television screens in a shop window along Croydon high street. There was a warm golden glow to the afternoon. It was night by the time the Kent countryside was receding into the distance. One stop at Sittingbourne is made to pick up a girl who lives here and she joins the rest of a party of twelve previous strangers including myself in a converted old ambulance as we head off into the big wide world. On the way down to the coast I notice a dark round object that goes bouncing and rolling away from us. This turns out to be a spare tyre and we hope this is not a bad omen.

Crossing the channel the air is cool on deck but the dawn brings a grey inanimate day as we move through cardboard stand-up toy looking towns. I eat an unappetising bowl of cereal I had brought along and eventually we join one of the endless autobahns that are tedium itself. At a break by a hotel in the country everyone goes into the bar but I feel the need to stretch my legs so climb a nearby hill. It is deceptively steep but once at the top the view is worth it as it is reminiscent of a Durer etching. Everything is very still and clear enabling a considerable vista.

Back on board we trundle on for several hours and the girl next to me leans her head on my shoulder to sleep. Come nightfall we pull into an area of homely looking fir-trees and in a clearing erect the three tents that the party possesses, mine being one of them. Three people is a bit of a jam in a tent designed for two. Austria is impressive, like being in a huge dramatic film set; amazing chocolate-box alpine houses with wide overhanging roofs and window-boxes filled with flowers. At night we camp underneath the shadow of an awesome looking mountain and boy is it cold. We all huddle up together but have only one sleeping-bag between three of us—once again mine! This is unzipped to its full width and we rely on body heat. Dancing about in the early morning sun we are glad to be on our way. Late in the afternoon the gloomy shadows spread across the valleys as we travel overnight. The following day is grey and overcast but turns to sun on entering Greece where a wayside stop is made. It is nicely rural and relaxed. I find a spot under the shade of a tree, lean back and bask under a warm blue sky and consume a bunch of grapes I've purchased. This is the life.

In the evening we pull up at a flat coastside area where there is a solitary taverna. There is a nice wide soft sandy beach. One of the girls goes for a dip while the rest of us buy bottles of drink which I get mixed up. Thinking what I have is Ouzo wine it turns out to be the stronger brandyish Raki. This after I have drunk about a bottle and a half in quick time. I have a sudden uncontrollable urge to swim across the Mediterranean and it takes the whole group to hold me down physically to persuade me otherwise.

The next thing I know an orb of gold surrounded by rays of light is looking down on me out of a sea of blue—one of the girls has looked in on me in the morning, having put up my tent and then me in it for the night. The sand is soft but the hangover is sledgehammer fashion. I make apologies all round and we hit the road.

That evening the land begins to rise and the road winds around hills with cypress-trees silhouetted against the sky. Then suddenly there is a descent and we enter Kavala, a sea resort. We stay here a few days, the most memorable experience for me being a visit to the washroom. On sitting down a lizard shoots up from the darkness, up my leg, the wall and out. I didn't use those facilities again but preferred to chance it in the open behind rocks.

I'm impatient to leave and am glad when we do so although I have to say that the peaches there were the best I'd ever had. Having crossed the Turkish border the land passed through now of 'Turkey in Europe' has that look to it of being neither of the East nor the West. Drawing near to Istanbul there will shortly be no doubt though as we enter the 'Gateway to the East'.

Resting up in a dormitory I take the opportunity to write a letter, giving a visit to a Turkish bath a miss. Next morning we wind our way through the narrow streets down to the ferry, passing a long queue of Americans applying for visas. The quayside was full of bustle and colour, crowded with people from all walks of life and amid the smell of sea air we boarded the packed ferry to cross the Bosphorus.

The temperature begins to increase as the miles start to stretch out and habitation becomes scarce as do trees and greenery. It dawns on me that I don't seem to consume much apart from some fruit and tea. That night is spent bivouacking in the rough and tumble of a roadside ditch. We are up early to the humming sound of traffic. The next night is spent in what looks like a bombed out building and we all spread out in the solitary first floor room. The walls vibrate all night as juggernauts thunder past. The movement on the bus becomes ceaseless and uneven. There is little conversation, people either dozing or daydreaming. At last at night we stop somewhere to eat. It turns out to be a wolf in sheep's clothing as the very greasy rice goes down well—too well. We are told there are bandits about so we are on the move all night. I think I'm beginning to lose weight with the incessant bumping, heat and lack of sleep.

Day brings barren rocky country where you can't even make out the track. My emotions have passed through stages of boredom, isolation and excitement. It is beginning to feel like true adventure. A descent is made from rocky hills to a flatter terrain where events take a serious turn. There's been an earthquake. We're in a remote area and villages have been reduced to rubble. I experience my first major culture shock realising we're definitely somewhere else now. The quake must have happened a few days or so ago.

Organisation and officialdom is conspicuous by its absence. Although on stopping we are put in the picture of what's happened by a local official. We are warned that we are into bandit country, armed robbers who would think nothing of leaving you dead in the middle of nowhere. Something you normally think of as fictional is reality. The advice is on no account stray from the main route, join a convoy and don't stop at night.

What really hit me was the sight of a young boy between about seven to ten years old who obviously hadn't eaten for days. There were no provisions and the locals had lost most possessions in the debris. He was gnawing a chunk of wood from the wreckage out of desperate hunger. But for the reality it was hard to conceive. If I was daydreaming before, I wasn't now, I was right on my toes. Being able to move out in the bus, thanks to modern technology, was a relief but I didn't forget the boy—nor ever will.

We have to stop for fuel. There is a nasty atmosphere from the locals—very hostile—it's the middle of the day and the sun is shining brightly. A further cultural realisation is that several of the girls on the bus have long blond hair. Most of the small crowd that gather round the bus in this village are male, no not most—all; mainly young. It dawns on me; this is a different way of life and natural curiosity on their part for apparitions sweeping in from another world.

Tension mounts, nobody has got out of the bus apart from the driver to refuel. The crowd, not satisfied with just peering in, start to physically rock the vehicle from side to side. Not before time the driver returns brandishing a wood-chopper and we make a hasty getaway. It is pretty hairy and nobody speaks for a while. Gradually the route becomes more even and the horizon broadens—there is a sense of quiet relief.

Then something happens I felt quite magical about, we are told by the archaeologist amongst us that we are soon to pass Mount Arrarat. Sure enough there shortly loomed the feature. Not physically impressive in itself. Distinct though in its solitary position on what amounts to a plain. It took a while to pass and we were reasonably close. One or two took photos. This is where Noah's Ark was supposed to have rested before the Flood receded.

One thing was for sure now, it was real hot during the day. You didn't need many clothes although it could get chilly at night. There followed a scenic interlude as the vastness of the landscape with its sense of exposure condensed into a less dramatic one. As the scale diminished a feeling of protection increased. The body became less tense and with it the mind. We came into a high river valley—gorge. Therefore we must previously have been on a plateau rather than plain. The sides were steep but not imposing and the floor was wide.

We stopped near a rope bridge. It was a fascinating sight strung out against the backdrop of the fast running shallow river. The span was wide and it looked precarious so no one tried to cross it. There were plenty of pebbles by the water's edge so you could get to drink easily—and oh what a drink; probably the first of its kind I'd ever had—clear cold fresh mountain water, after days of non-stop travel, dust and heat, also a proper wash, quite something for me at that time. We ate some unleavened bread with goats cheese and someone asked me why I was a vegetarian which seemed a superfluous question under the circumstances.

The river began to deepen and drop away as the road hugged the climbing hillside. Some greenery and trees became visible for the first time in ages—it sprang up beside the widening river and as the route ascended could be seen below. Then a weird spine-chilling sound was heard. Everyone stared at each other as from a reasonable distance although obviously within earshot came a tremendous deep roar seeming to echo out of some timeless dark cavernous depth. I had never heard anything like it. It was like something from the dawn of creation. In due course it was discovered to be a mountain leopard.

The nights were warm now so you could sleep in your bag under the stars. They had great clarity and seemed nearer. We came into a hot deep trail next day. The colours and outlines of shapes appearing vivid with a dreamlike quality. Stopping in the main street of a small town I was stood a chai by a travelling anthropologist. Although this was a foreign environment there was an intimate sense of security. As a snake sheds its skin I was shaking mine, letting go and really beginning to travel.

As I was to discover later we were passing through a district of Armenia, the notion of which had always intrigued me, the reality being no let down. There was a vague romance to the area.

The Iranian border is approached. The former name of Persia had poetical associations which was born out to an extent by the view from the broadening sweep of road, high above occasional oases. The sight of a crashed truck at the bottom of a ravine serves to bring back the reality of the modern world. The town of Tabriz is reached.

Then come long days constantly moving in an unchanging landscape. It feels like shrinking into an ever-expanding horizon. Eventually to the north appear, as if a backdrop to a stage or film set, a vast range of dimple-folded purple mountains. They must be real but don't look it.

We enter the wide streets of Tehran and park in a side-alley. I stay in the bus with the children while the others go roaming. Men sit outside chai-shops and talk. As darkness descends we make a trip to the top floor of a sky-scraper hotel. We move out next day and a period of calm ensues.

The gleaming turquoise mosaic of a domed mosque is sighted and the people in the winding street look at us with gazing wonder.

We have a flat tyre so everyone piles out to give a hand as traffic whizzes by. Stuck for a while in the middle of nowhere toiletry is a bit of a problem. Away from the main highway which is now smoothly tarmacked there are boulders to go behind. Whilst on such a visit a dreadful thought occurs to me. Imagine returning to find the wheel having been fixed and the bus gone without anyone noticing your absence. I speeded up my operations and returned to find things just as I had left them.

Suddenly—Meshad, the last main town in Iran before Afghanistan. There is a large swimming pool here which is a great relief. The Afghan border is something. On one side nothing—on the other a medieval fortress. There is no accommodation and the ground is too hard for tents so we sleep on top of the bus as there are wild dogs roaming. Before doing this I go to find food without success and on coming back take the wrong direction. Suddenly I'm stopped by a gleaming fixed bayonet pointing straight at me inches away in the darkness. A border-guard, who clearly doesn't understand English. "Tourist, English," I say, panicking and putting my hands up in the air. He seems placated and I turn back. A scary moment when time stood still for a few seconds.

Once through the border it really is out into the wilderness. Brown and barren as far as the eye can see. The bus is a speck in the vastness. An even smaller speck is passed—a solitary cyclist! He looks Japanese, has strands of black hair hanging down under his floppy sun-hat and his bike is loaded down with saddlebags. Eventually we arrive at the town of Herat.

Enter a new world. Hardly any motor traffic and not many females. It fascinates me to see men on horseback, gigs drawn by horses with plumage in daily use. Good single-storey accommodation is found. Spacious rooms, sound beds, reasonably priced and also a garden with a pelican wandering around. The first night is rest. Like getting off a roundabout you've been on too long it's pure bliss to sleep on a bed and in a room that isn't bumping and moving after so many nights constant travelling.

Next day to get some clothes. Walking down the street is an experience. The men wearing turbans or scull caps, dark beards or long white ones, all in colourful clothing. They walk slowly due to the heat and do not seem to see me. I am invisible. By contrast the rare women are covered from head to foot in full black purdah with only a face-gauze to see through and go scurrying like mice to and fro on their errands.

I pass a beautiful domed mosque with its full lapis lazuli colour shining in the sun. On reaching a commercial area I locate a clothes booth run by a boy. There are no prices and we haggle. He is a sharp business boy. The best ploy I tried, without thinking, is to walk away. He comes running after me to accept my last offer. I get a baggy pair of lime-green pyjama bottoms. I already have a cheesecloth top. My plimsolls make up the full regalia.

To eat I get what looks like some chick-pea soup from a street vendor, tasty, but might not stay down. I then go to get some Afghan money. I have split from the rest of the party with two others, a Spanish girl and English husband, as we think the others' hotel too commercial even though they have showers that don't work. All the toilets by now are just holes in the ground. For luxury you get feet grips. These did not stop me coming a cropper in Tehran—although I still slept with two girls that night as the heat did its drying work! Tonight us three smoke in the tent which we've put up by the garden wall—a bit strange. The next night I head to an upstairs joint with carpets and cushions, live music with a tabla and homemade looking sitar-type instrument. There is a hookah and travellers from all over. Really great, never felt so alive.

Herat is left behind and as we're leaving who should we see coming into town? The Japanese cyclist! I am the only one of the party in native dress—I figured if locals wear it then it's the most suitable for the climate. Sure enough after looks of both approval and mirth whilst most others sweat in Levis I'm pretty cool.

Until now between the isolated small settlements camels could be seen, some wild. Others were in gatherings of black-clad people grouped together around vast tents—Bedouins. Now there is nothing in sight at all. One of the most memorable parts of the trip for me. Strange windblown rock formations abound—eroded into the most weird and wonderful shapes. Initially it's a bit like moving through a huge modern sculpture exhibition but then as it goes on and the scale increases is more like I imagine it would be riding in a moon-buggy. It really does seem like you could be on another planet. Although there are no craters you could easily think this was the moon.

With not only the long distances involved it is also Ramadan, where fasting is observed during the daylight hours, so opportunities for obtaining food are even scarcer. A chai-shop during the day sells just that. We do come at night however to a welcoming compact town no more the size of an overgrown village really but buzzing with life. Kerosene lamps everywhere, huge bread-ovens emitting captivating smoky baking smells. The unleavened bread is fresh, cheap and plentiful.

Also on the streets, something that was to become a regular for me, vendors cooking corn on the cob over an open charcoal fire. A good food as no oil or fat involved. The fruit stalls are also impressive. Multicoloured displays, most of the contents unknown to me. I know the pomegranates though with their crimson beaded sparkling interiors. They made a welcome change from the many truck-stop water-melon stalls frequently passed on the open road, piled high black and green stripy mounds, one or two cut to reveal their watery red, black-pip studded interiors to entice the thirsty traveller.

Although it is very hot now it is dry heat and after a period of adjustment I find it thoroughly enjoyable. The blue skies and sunshine give a zest to life bringing a brightness and clarity of outline as in Technicolor film. With the general absence of vegetation colours stand out more. If there were visitors from this land to a jungle no doubt they would find the contrast equally striking.

Even the nights on the move have an almost vivid quality. The altitude is higher so I guess this could be a reason for the stars appearing brighter. Also this is a huge land with no railways, few motor vehicles and little heavy industry so pollution is low if not in Western terms non-existent. Only a small amount of minerals are to be found here. Whether this is seen as favourable or not it has meant that change has been superficial. The country is geographically strategic in its position between central and southern Asia.

Kandahar is reached in the dead of night. Only of course this is when it comes to life. It is one of three main towns and lies at the bottom of an upside down triangle on the main route. To the north is the virtually uninhabited central region and it is separated from Pakistan and the Arabian sea to the south by a range of mountains which are the tail end of the Hindu Kush. The middle of nowhere but important for its position on the route.

An aspect of the people that I admired was that they were fervent in their religious practice and beliefs and also tolerant of outsiders. I was starting to view life in different ways. Having only Western concepts as points of reference I found this fascinating and opening up a broader outlook. For instance, what I traditionally understood as hospitality was being pressed on me by an almost gushing form of friendliness, food, drink and comfort. I came to feel that although I was a foreigner I had freedom of movement. No particular demands were made except for finance apart from which the attitude was live and let live.

Pulling up for fuel on the outskirts of Kandahar I received an unfortunate baptism. Seeking a place to answer the call of nature and not fully grasping the fact that in a short distance from the bus it becomes pitch-black, due to lack of street lighting, I went astray. Sanitary piping is virtually nonexistent here, the sewers are open trenches at the side of the road. The rest is left to the imagination. Suffice to say I experienced a warm wet feeling in the dark up to my waist. I was not flavour of the month back on the bus. I couldn't help grinning though.

Into town, which if anything looks even more Wild West than Herat, and longed-for rest. The stop is not lengthy. On we go. The scenery still rugged and the altitude increasing. A striking change occurs in the constitution of the road surface. At an arbitrary juncture it alters from the concrete associated with old airfields where there is a rumple sound at regular laying intervals, to the continuous smooth surface of tarmac.

There is a marked difference in travel comfort from the bone-shaking, spine-crunching of the former which ruins suspension of body and vehicle, to the featherbed feel of the latter which in comparison, coupled with the conjoined cessation of sound-effects, feels like floating on air. It's akin to a toothache you've become used to suddenly vanishing. Just as suddenly, a long distance later, this also comes to an abrupt end, presumably when the black stuff ran out—or maybe the greenback stuff.

More long hours of semi-wilderness and then Kabul is arrived at. This is the capital and larger than anywhere else but still by Western standards really only a very large town. Initially it has a more modern feel; an airport and more bustle. However this is really only superficial.

Another welcome rest was spent lazing around a small hotel. It is about five thousand feet above sea-level here so felt fresher and the heat not so intense as in Kandahar. The hotel had a homely feel with pleasant gardens. There was more variety of food with good salads although a bit more expensive. I made one or two forays during the day and at night but in truth I was now eager to move on.

Now I had arrived at the point that this whole trip was all about. Over the distant horizon lay my destination. I had a subconscious sixth sense about this. Right at the end of the Himalayan range it felt that 'over the hill' was a different scene. I was feeling in good shape passing through Jalalabad. Moving at good speed, the air was fresh and clear, the sky was blue, the mountain rocks vivid. Several of us looked at each other with a knowing grin. This was it.

II. OVER

AS THE WINDING DESCENT began my ears popped, as in a tunnel or aeroplane, giving an added sense of occasion as all sounds were vague and distant. The gorge of the Khyber Pass began to open up. Instead of being able to see far-flung mountain ranges the rock walls on either side steepen. As the track wound even more a sheer drop to the left became deeper and deeper. A track was all it was. Hardly wide enough to pass an oncoming vehicle in many places driving here is a thin line between being exciting and frightening. The native bus and lorry drivers have a different concept of highway code, namely survival. It appears more like the attitude of the dodgems at the fairground.

The serious difference is the evidence of casualties lying at the bottom of the gorge. It is quite commonplace to see crashed vehicles littered about where the road and them have parted company. There are no crash barriers and frequent rockfalls are a constant hazard. Being seated on the outside part of the vehicle really is very hairy.

The most colourful feature at this stage are the local public buses. They are incredibly decorated as if in a carnival with painted patterns and designs, tinsel and silver. They are always packed out with passengers and luggage of all manner and description. People travel on the roof and actually hang on to the back and outside, some with nothing between them and a drop of hundreds of feet; nothing is thought of this at all! Once the first culture shock is overcome it is a sight never forgotten.

The pass gradually begins to widen out and the shear rock faces recede and broaden. This leads to the North-West Frontier—the Pakistan border. It feels like going back in time. There is what looks like the ruins of a large fort and it is one of the busiest borders. Everywhere men are milling about carrying ancient looking rifles and have bandoleers slung over their shoulders. The atmosphere is dustier and the smells more pungent as impromptu fires and camps are set up for the night ready to pass through in the morning. Landi Kotal is immediately over the border, the first railway station into Pakistan. It took a whole day to come down the pass and I felt as if I had completed the first stage of entering a new world.

Up to this point in time there had been a long metamorphosis of culture and language. I relied mainly on sign-language which is understood quite readily. From now on I surprised myself by feeling strange to speak English again and be commonly understood. It seemed like a weird anticlimax in a way to have come so far and through so much and then have the almost cosy feeling of speaking native language. But English is only the second language and there are a myriad of local dialects.

Coming into Pakistan our passports are stamped efficiently and as we queue various less official looking gentlemen inquire if we would be interested in obtaining certain commodities. We shake our heads in the negative. Foreign currency is obtained for the penultimate time. My American Express traveller's cheques have stretched further as the journey has gone on. I really spend little money. There is no dramatic change in the first parts of the country. There are less turbans worn and it feels hotter. Then gradually appears that which normally I take for granted but seem to have almost forgotten—green vegetation. It is like a black and white film turning to colour. You know you are now somewhere different.

The city of Peshawar is entered at night, teeming with life and steaming hot. You can hardly move in the markets and it appears a centre of organised chaos. The next day feels less oppressive. Through Pakistan we do a fair bit of night travelling although there is a driving rest spent stationary in the middle of nowhere. We are on the roof again to avoid trouble in the middle of which night the sky, mountains in the distance and everything around is lit up by fantastic sheets of white light without any sound. A spectacular electric storm.

Good time is made to the Indian border. As with all borders there are two sides—one for each country and a small no-mans land in between. It helps to get through at least one of these at night if not both because they can be time-consuming and if you want to set off next day, it is frustrating if you arrive just after they've closed which is about sundown. All you can do is twiddle your thumbs (or anything else) till the next day. On this occasion we managed to scrape through the first side by way of a shameful bribe—whisky is apparently high currency—we were leaving a Muslim area and entering the Punjab. However that was it for the night.

Conditions told us we were now in India. We could stroll about a bit but not wander too far. It was a lovely evening. The sun had not in fact quite gone down. Native boys—really dark skinned with shiny black hair were bathing naked and playing in a nearby water pump. Water-buffaloes were cooling off in water-hollows. These hollows led into irrigation channels and out into the fields. In a way although inland it had the look of a coastal scene with sand dunes. This was enhanced by the tall light-green grass giving the whole scene a fresh feel. It was also the effect of water after so much dust and heat. I took a bathe myself.

We were kindly allowed to sleep in the customs-building, but wait, sudden shouting, gesticulating and panic—no, no, no—must not sleep on floor—snakes. There were raised stone slabs in the room which looked like experimentation tables in a chemistry laboratory, in reality used for checking luggage through; these were not comfortable but safe. No one moved off these till morning.

When morning came our efforts of the previous evening bore fruit in that if we had needed to go through both sides of the border that day I doubt if we would have made it. As it was we only had one to go through, which was still lengthy. However this turned out to be very pleasant for although hardly any distance from where we were the previous evening there was a spacious picnic area with shady trees.

It was while waiting here I realised how much I had missed the variety of shape and colour that the trees provided. In addition there was the new sight of groups of families sitting around with women in brightly coloured saris amongst them. I felt this cultural difference in the relaxed social atmosphere with which I was familiar.

At last it was time to hit the road, the Grand Trunk Road. As we moved along wide green flat fields could be seen interspersed between the trees that line the side of the road.

Travelling was reasonably smooth considering the conglomeration of road users: pedestrians, cyclists, oxen pulling carts, scooters, the familiar public buses now done out Hindi-style according to which deity was worshipped there would be appropriate decorations in the front; animals everywhere, cows roaming, wild dogs, monkeys, poultry—a casual flowing mayhem. There were mainly Sikhs but also Hindus wearing white loin-cloths called dhotis. The population was definitely larger here and there was greater activity between the towns.

Pulling up at a modern looking hotel for the night the air was steaming and humid after recent rainfall. I wandered into the street where there were various food stalls selling dahl, samosas, sweetstuffs and allsorts. A good choice for a vegetarian and I got a lot for my rupees. Also has some good hot tea. I'd succumbed in the heat to a few Cokes and Fantas which don't really quench your thirst at all. There was a verandah outside the bedroom on the first floor so after noshing I went and sat up there to relax and survey the brightly lit busy scene. After a while the Aussie girl with us came out and had a chat. She was making her way back to Oz so we would soon be parting.

The town was Amritsar so next morning I took a taxi to the Golden Temple and walked out to the amazing place in the middle of a lake. You walk on a long connecting narrow pier almost level with the water and then come back the same way on a one-way system. It is an intricate white square building tipped with gold. With plimsolls removed I paid a visit. This is the centre for Sikh pilgrimage. Not being a Sikh I thought it very open and generous-spirited that I could go there quite freely. In Amritsar I got my first real sight of begging in India. I did not know quite what to make of it at first. The amount of crippled beggars, most of all those with amputated limbs on home-made skate-board affairs came as a shock. I was to discover that some parents actually had this done to their children in order to send them out to beg. A sad but real fact of life most prominent in the big cities.

My spontaneous emotion to this was of heart-breaking pity. My head pretty quickly pointed out to me though that apart from being on a relative shoe-string myself I would have to be the World Bank if I gave to every beggar, therefore as I couldn't give to one and not another I had to be hard and not give at all. Henceforth this gave me a rather cynical attitude to life but a necessary one for survival. A similar code had applied in Turkey, Iran and Afghanistan, only with street urchins—if you gave backsheesh to one, which you were always being asked, the next minute you'd be descended on by thirty or more out of nowhere, which you'd have a real job shaking off. Rule—don't do it.

Now came a long last leg to Delhi before resting up. A virtually non-stop haul was made to get there. The heat had become even more intense and by the time the outskirts were reached it felt as if my blood was beginning to boil. I was actually going through a period of aclimatisation and pretty soon began to enjoy it. We arrived in Delhi at night, stopping in a central parking and camping area which was a sort of compound. Therefore nothing really had been seen of the city. Everyone was pretty exhausted so the first night's sleep was a good one. I then found out the idea was to stay here for a while. The trip was scheduled to go on to Goa. This was now a watershed for me. Although all the others seemed content with this situation and just to hang around this site eating the not authentically local food and talking about not very much—I was not.

There had been scattered occasions en route when I had wanted to move on but it had not been feasible. Money had been paid up front so it had not been logical to go independent and spend more on local transport. To be fair it had also literally been foreign to me. The couple I hung out with in Herat had also been frustrated which was why us three found a cheaper hotel. The driver obviously got to stay gratis at certain places on route in return for providing steady custom. Now we were in India and relatively near the end I felt differently. I had achieved my first objective—to get to the sub-continent. From what I had heard the railway system here was cheap and extensive. So I was going to split.

This was just as much an instinctive decision as a thought out one. I went around to see the others and make farewells. The archaeologist had got off in Tehran, heading south; I couldn't find the American and his designer clothes English girlfriend. She had kindly lent me her sunglasses and he I had found extraordinary in that he was a ventriloquist and had actually brought his dummy with him, even giving us a demo in Kabul!

I had already spoken to lady Oz. The Scottish bloke was on his back, ill, maybe a touch of sunstroke as he was near enough bald and had lapsed in wearing his sun-hat a couple of times but more likely he was just having a deal of trouble with the heat—his white skin had gone red underneath his T-shirt. He was a nice bloke but I had wondered what such a relatively conservative person was doing on a trip like this. The girls were looking after him, especially I think the Scottish Cambridge twins (known as such from their prior place of residence). I didn't say a lot but wished them well. I then parted with the others.

My Herat friends were planning on doing the same thing in a day or two and thought I was making a good move. We parted warmly. I was expecting the last part to be a bit emotional as I had slept with them and we had been through a lot. But it was quiet, a mixture of both sad and inevitable. We hardly spoke. No exchange of addresses in England. No plans to meet up. I don't remember their names. They were both blond, medium height and young. The one from Wimbledon was plumper and a good swimmer. I was close to her. The other one was from Sittingbourne—Kent, pretty, quieter. I never forgot them and still love them.

I didn't tell the people on the bus, I just walked out of the site gates and into India.

III. IN ELYSIUM

AS I WALKED OUT INTO The wide street I realised that for the first time I was truly on my own. In the middle of a huge foreign city with no contacts at all this might have seemed daunting. On the contrary I felt a great sense of freedom and excitement. The lulled lethargy that had started to creep over me in the last day or two was replaced by a great rush of energy and sense of adventure.

The most logical thought that came into my mind was to locate a railway station. I obtained directions easily. The language situation was now no problem. Names and signs were now in both Sanskrit and English. I felt a virtual sense of luxury in this. I could have got one of hundreds of three-wheeler black and yellow taxis that swarm around but after days on my backside I enjoyed walking and was able to take in the scene. There was a terrific commotion as masses of people jostle to and fro. The atmosphere was hot and dusty with pungent smells hitting you at every turn—not all of them savory.

It took a while for me to get used to the idea that just answering a call of nature by the side of the road, squat fashion, is accepted behaviour. As in every city in India there is a great cacophony of sound—not only of people—monkeys, dogs, cows and buffalo roam everywhere. The traffic noise and chaos is initially unbelievable; jammed buses, taxis, bicycles, scooters, pedestrians—you name it—with no sense of order. To me it was a miracle how anyone ever got anywhere. After a while however you realise that this is all normal part and parcel of life here.

In due course I arrived at the station. As I was about to find out the railways are a unique institution. There never was a better demonstration of organised chaos. It is both bewildering and charming. How to figure out what was going where and when I was at a complete loss, so I just joined one of the many long queues at random. These all led to a wide grilled bar similar in look to an old fashioned bank in an American Western film. As yet I had no idea of the pricing variation so in my mind I had plumped for third-class.

There are actually four classes: first you get a private compartment; second is normal carriage but more or less reserved seats; third is—I don't think there's a description for third, you just jam in wherever you can; the unofficial fourth is—hanging on to the side or on the roof—fourth is free. I got to the grille and discovered that booking your ticket, particularly on a longish journey, needs to be done quite a bit in advance. This is something of a bureaucratic farce when it comes to third-class because basically it's everyone for themselves when the time comes. However I said I wanted to go to Bombay. The next departure was not for eight hours which I had to settle for. But what amazed me was how little it cost, no more than a few pounds sterling.

I thought to myself that I'd be able to travel all over without breaking the bank. To the average Indian the cost would seem more which is why fourth-class is a popular choice. The journey was to take thirty-six hours. I had done plenty of overnight travel sleeping by now but hadn't bargained on the hard seats. I walked outside for a bit and watched one of the dozens of makeshift cricket games going on in a nearby park. As I now had to lug my sleeping bag and tent around with me in my rucksack I wasn't going very far in the sun. I also had to keep close to my rucksack as one disadvantage of my clothing was that I had no pockets, so passport, train tickets and money had to be kept in it. After a while I invented a Heath Robinson method of stashing this inside the cord that held up my pyjama trousers.

I decided to spend the rest of the wait back at the station. From what I could make out it was the main terminus for central and southern destinations. It was a large building and I found a choice of two restaurants, North Indian or Southern. The North Indian was busier and on investigation I discovered that there were more meat-orientated dishes. The customers were a mixture of Muslim, Hindi and Sikh.

The Southern restaurant was a different ballgame altogether and really attracted me. For a start there was an air of almost deserted tranquillity about it. There were far less customers, virtually all of whom were of much slighter stature than in the Northern. It was also strictly vegetarian. As a vegetarian this meant a far wider choice for me. Also it was much hotter and spicier. What you call the real McCoy.

I sampled all sorts of dishes the content of which I hadn't a clue. There's no cutlery, you just use chapatis to scoop the sauces and mixtures from metal bowls or use fingers, a cultural nuance I soon adapted to. This is practically the case everywhere east of Istanbul. I have to admit this leaves a bit to be desired hygienewise. Then came one of those moments that always stay with you. I had been quite blasé, about choosing the food, not paying too much detailed attention as it was all so incredibly cheap—about fifteen pence I'd reckoned.

I had sat down and started to eat hungrily. The tables and chairs were well spaced, the nearest person being about ten feet from me. I suddenly hit something—hot. I thought a firework had gone off inside me. I couldn't move. My mouth was wide open and I didn't know where to look for embarrassment. Real tears started to roll down my cheeks and I felt genuinely ashamed of myself. Of course no one was actually looking at me. I must have cried for several minutes. Until then I hadn't known anything edible could be that strong. After a while I recovered and had learnt another lesson—be on guard when eating.

I then went down to the platform where a striking sight is all the official porters gathered around squatting in their self-made enclosure waiting for a long-distance arrival. They all wear deep-maroon clothing, both tops and bottoms. The colour is strong so the dye must be of a high quality. The amounts and size of luggage they carry is truly amazing. To me the temperature was sweltering but to them it was a way of life. They still didn't have my envy. Without any form of mechanical aides such as trolleys or push carriers all forms of goods are hauled about. I saw one porter with three huge trunks carried on his head! A lot of them wear large deep crocus-yellow turbans—this to protect from heat, absorb perspiration and as I saw most practically, to balance huge trunks on.

I am not a railway buff but the sight of some of the enormous engines shunting in and out of sidings does have a unique atmosphere. Quite a few are old-fashioned steam which was something I only saw as a small boy. Of course there is noise and grime everywhere but I found it fun. When the massive wheels start to move and the pistons pump you can feel the power. The amount of people on the platform began to swell, the porters began to stir, hawkers started to appear. I sensed the arrival of my train was imminent.

In due course it was difficult to move and the general clamour rose to a crescendo as the train pulled in. I had no idea whether it was on time or not but the general idea was to look for a carriage with the alphabetical letter that tallied with that on my ticket. I soon gave that up as a lost cause. The more practical pursuit seemed to be of joining in what to all intents and purposes looked like a rugby scrum. I was not in altogether a bad position for this because I am fairly tall, especially in comparison with a lot of the natives, so here's for it, head down and charge.

A few minutes later I am in a corridor, then a compartment and jam myself down on a seat next to the window. I say window, they are open spaces with bars across them. If the bars are to prevent people climbing in and out if you are either small or determined enough they don't do the job. The seats are hard wooden benches so I got my sleeping-bag to sit on. The carriage then became completely packed. There are no airs and graces for women or the elderly—the law of nature applies—where there is a space, fill it. What I noticed through all this was there was not the slightest sign of irritability or anger on the part of anyone despite the pushing, shoving and general scrambling for position. As if by magic once the compartment was full all the commotion evaporated and a sense of calm pervaded the air. However when I say full, I mean it. The benches were squashed, people stood between them and the luggage-racks weren't used just for luggage.

At first I had felt a smug sense of satisfaction in obtaining a place but this was replaced by impatience as the train then remained in the station for at least a couple of hours. No one else showed any sign of frustration. I was beginning to understand that the concept of time and the pace of life in the Orient are altogether different than in the Occident.

During this time vendors were constantly going up and down the platform selling hot snacks, fruit and drink. The most common was the 'chai' wallah. The repetitious call of "chai de chai" echoing into the dusk at regular intervals. The price of chai is virtually give away. The wallah carries a huge stack of throw away clay bowls in one arm and a great kettle of ready-made steaming hot sweet tea with the other. He has the knack of pouring this and taking money as well. It is the most refreshing drink to have. As I was next to the window there was an almost continual flow of commodities passing by me into the compartment and corridor.

The people, some on their own, others in family groups, and all what is seen as peasants, were very friendly towards me which was a nice feeling as if I was one of them. I had thought about gong to Agra to visit the Taj Mahal while I was in Delhi but decided against it on the basis that it would be crawling with tourists. By this time I could have been and come back again as it was now night. Then at last another commotion stirred on the platform heralding departure and slowly but surely objects on the station started to move and I was leaving Delhi as I had come—by night.

There was little breeze despite the movement of the train as we trundled out through the suburbs; lights flickered everywhere in the warm darkness, gradually dwindling in number until the complete blanket of night said that Delhi had been left behind. Kerosene-lamps illuminated outlying local stations and small villages in the distance, stars began to come out in the sky, inside the train, in thick yellow light, food was still being consumed everywhere but the general hubbub had died down and with the hypnotic 'clickiti click-clackati clack' of the wheels on the track I fell into the arms of Morpheus.

"Chai de Chai!"... "Chai de Chai!"I woke with a start. I was greeted with the image of two gleaming eyes and a keyboard of teeth as a chai wallah pressed himself into the opening next to me. A night time stop had been made. There was activity everywhere reminiscent of rush hour at a main line terminus. I had not expected this, thinking the journey would be non-stop. However, as there were going to be a few stops I took the opportunity to have a chai and samosa. The constant dry heat was certainly giving me a thirst and at the equivalent of about an old halfpenny this was just the job.

We moved off again and for quite a while I stayed awake just gazing into the night. I did doze for a while eventually. When I came to a grey light had started to creep over the countryside. Shapes of trees began to appear out of a vale of mist which hung in strips over the scattered water-hollows and irrigation channels. The deep-orange ball of the sun emerged on the horizon and a new day was beginning as I entered the heart of central India.

A common tree in this area is the banyan which has characteristic horizontal branches and spidery foliage. On closer inspection it is seen to be a favourite haunt of monkeys. People start to work in the fields early and the ubiquitous water-buffalo is to be seen but the frantic motion of the city has been left far behind. The train moves at a steady pace—I guess not doing more than fifty miles per hour and the fastest thing passed is the odd cyclist.

As the long hours stretch out it becomes hot in the flat landscape. The main buildings of any substance are the rural train stations looking slightly incongruous set in isolation. There are no raised platforms outside the cities (even these are not high) so movable wooden steps are sometimes seen but mainly it‘s a question of clambering up and down from the carriages. A lot of the village buildings are straw-roofed huts. Others are constructed with well made brick, being a mixture of dried cow dung and straw, then the outside is whitewashed. The roofs are generally flat as opposed to the pitched ones of the lesser buildings.

At one stop I got off to stretch my legs. The engine was taking on water which is a long procedure so I had no worry about being stranded. The people were very friendly and one family invited me in for tea. They were curious to know about England and the outside world which was just as strange and remote to them as this was to me.

I found it fascinating rather than strange and felt naturally at ease in the environment. Each family has its own private domestic shrine where daily devotions take place with mantras chanted. There is usually a small white-cloth-covered table on which an image of the local deity is placed with flowers and perhaps dishes of sweetstuffs. Incense is burned which helps keep flies at bay. There is little or no furniture as people are used to sitting cross-legged.

Back on board we now started to enter a central desert region with hardly any vegetation and only remote villages. The sun was scorching and I drifted off into a hazy sleep. When I awoke I took another big upward step on my learning curve. Initially I was pleased to see the colourful scenery around me; there was more foliage outside, densely packed and closer to the carriage. One or two passengers half-smiled at me. Then I became aware of a strange nauseous sensation. I felt vaguely dizzy and weak.

Glancing about me I had a mild shock. Before going to sleep, which I did for about three hours, I had leant my right arm on the window-ledge. The sun had come round fully on that side of the carriage. My arm now resembled something like a dried up overdone roast chicken wing. The skin on the forearm was all shrivelled and when I moved it inside onto my lap it was really painful. It was too sore to touch and in places it had cracked and blistered. I had not realised the power of the sun in this climate and now understood why people covered up so much. I had rolled up the sleeves of my cheesecloth top for the last time.

After a stop where I consumed several bowls of tea I gradually felt better as the blood circulation improved. Having been drained in one sense I now felt the need for another. This is not an expedition lightly undertaken. In fact I think anyone completing the course should be awarded either a certificate or medal. What I'm talking about is a visit to the W.C. Sparing the graphic details I'll leave those inclined to their imaginations.

An official now appeared who must have the most thankless task imaginable—a ticket-inspector. Although train travel seemed cheap to me to country people a long-distance ticket might amount to several weeks wages. There was a form of gainful occupation undertaken by children in this part of the world. They ran alongside the train when it slowed at a bend, jumped on it, then went from carriage to carriage begging, then hopped off.

I admired their energy and even though they were obviously poor they did all this with a mischievous sense of fun oblivious of the danger in their hazardous occupation. I caught the look in the eyes of one of these children as the doleful look designed to induce pity, thence cash, changed in a flash to a sense of glee and play-acting. I was tempted to give them something out of admiration rather than pity.

Day passed again into night and I slept pretty well. The scheduled thirty-six hour journey should have meant arriving in Bombay about eight in the morning. Nothing doing. The sun beat down on a vast plain as midday approached. The wooden seats and sleeping slumped in a corner was beginning to stiffen me up. So, braving the assault course, I decided that some form of movement was required. I made my way along the corridor to the end of the carriage and managed to get myself a space by the door opening. The doors are always wide open. This is a less stifling place to be as although it is hot dusty air there is movement. A bit like having a hairdryer set on warm blown on your face in a sauna.

I squatted down right by the entrance where I got a really good view of the scenery as it rolled by. If I leaned my head slightly I could also see how precariously the free-riders travelled. One arm is hooked through one of the bars of a window and that's about the size of it. I could only marvel at the tenacity of these people to endure this for any length of time. At one stop when I only just got back on as the train started to move I got a sight of the roof-travellers. These people really are taking their lives into their hands but make themselves quite at home with little camps, food and drink.

In the middle of my ponderings I had not really taken much notice of a person sitting on the floor opposite me even though there was barely a foot separating us. I now did so. Dressed in long saffron robes with a long white beard was a sadhu, a travelling holy man. They are high in the caste system. Having renounced worldly affairs and possessions they are occupied in religious pilgrimage. They sleep where they can, often in temples or their precincts. Frequently they will be seen roof travelling rather than deny a person with a ticket a seat. It is seen as a duty to give them food as they are not like beggars in that they don't handle money. I had deduced he was a sadhu by the third eye painted on his forehead and the religious beads he wore. As we sat there we caught each other's eye. After passing a friendly smile I was quite taken back when he spoke to me in perfect English. He wanted to know where I was from and what I was doing. By this time, apart from the long beard, I was looking almost native myself. I told him what my general situation was and how I had arrived there.

He seemed amazed at first and then we had an interesting conversation for at least a couple of hours about philosophy and life in general. I think what caught his humour was my youth, he being I should say twenty or thirty years older than me. I was glad to have made this chance meeting and on parting we exchanged good wishes.

At last during the afternoon the outskirts of Bombay were reached. Thousands upon thousands of country people migrate to the city, being a huge international shipping port and trading centre which was even more important before the days of air travel, looking for work. The result is that vast shanty areas swell out from the suburbs where people have to endure not only poverty which they have thought to better themselves of but also the filth, squalor and disease which arise from their living conditions. They actually beg in groups. It is truly pitiful here as they clearly haven't got a hope. I did not plan to stay here.

On emerging into central Bombay my first requirement was to stretch for a bit. I went to one of the many fruit sellers near the station. You could get fresh coconut juice. The coconuts are not the small round brown hairy things seen at shies. They are smooth large rugby ball shaped and lime-green. The stall-holder has a broad-bladed chopper and with one swift stroke removes the top. You then drink the clear liquid straight from the remaining bowl. It was pleasant.

In a short distance I came to the main bus station. I discovered there was a bus leaving for Goa in two hours so I booked a ticket. It was another overnight job, twenty-four hours this time. With only a short wait I did not wander far but one thing I noticed was that Bombay seemed to be the national centre for the spitting of red ' beetlenut juice' on the ground. The first time I'd seen this I'd thought it was the result of some acute dental problem. You live and learn.

I boarded the bus in good time. After so long on a train it seemed strange. There was hardly any leg room and if possible it appeared even more packed. However I had got a window (no panes again) seat once more and was eager for the off. It was about six o' clock when we pulled out of the station and through the streets of Bombay. This form of locomotion was more intimate in a way as we were subject to the vagaries of the road and everything of it. The sights and smells came literally crowding in.

There was none of the assured steady progress of a railway track. Nevertheless within reasonable time the city was again left behind and I once more felt that sense of calm relief to be away from all the turmoil. Also we began to climb slowly into the hills towards Poona which was used as a hill-station by the British. The air became fresher, the country spread out, the vegetation was richer in colour and density. This was now in the tropic of Cancer. I nodded off—pleased to have made it thus far.

We were now high up into the range of hills that bestride the western coast of Southern India named the Western Ghats. Poona was passed during the night in my sleep. When I awoke the temperature was perfect, a really warm sunny morning with clear fresh air. It was like waking into another world. This was also true from a scenic point of view as the surroundings were now luxuriant forest jungle.

It was the first time in my life I had ever been in such an environment and it struck me as having the appearance of a kind of paradise. The lushness and variety of foliage intermingled with all description of wild flower, the slightly roller-coaster course of the road giving interchangeable views of distant forest roofs and crests, to then turn a corner and swoop into a tunnel of dark green with splashes of sunlight flecking through inside the bus, to emerge again to see a valley gorge below; I felt this all quite magical. I had no real sense of time as in a dreamlike quality.

The journey carried on like this with occasional stops. About midday a stop was made at a small village. The bus was not plied with hawkers at stops but there were still beggars which I had assumed was confined to the cities. One particularly frail and elderly woman was really persistent, going from window to window in a forlorn mechanical wraithlike manner. My temporary illusion of paradise was brought down to earth, because although I had seen worse in the cities I found this sight of destitution in the midst of the apparent abundance of nature far more distressing. It was with a real wrench that I inclined my head the other way when she was at my window, feeling a sense of selfish inhumanity. The picture of her face, with sunken cheeks and the outstretched arms seemingly thin and brittle as twigs, stays in my memory to this day.

The bus, unlike the train, was roughly on time despite several unscheduled stops in the country. We gradually began to come down from the hills and into Goa in the late afternoon. The first thing that struck me was the sprinkling of very well constructed bungalows, more like villas, with proper red undulating tiled roofs. I realised that this was an inheritance from the days when Goa was a Portuguese colony. After travelling through forest jungle you could almost feel as well as see the organised and formal air of colonial civilisation. They were beautiful buildings and blended in with surroundings harmoniously.

Through a few streets and into an open square the bus station of Panjim, the main town, was reached. The scale was small and relaxing and although it was only early evening I decided to look for accommodation and rest up. I was able to do this quickly and easily. A hotel just off the square provided dormitory sleeping quarters and had a modest restaurant. I was getting used to the idea that this only cost about twenty pence.

The layout which was on the first floor was reasonably spacious. There was a verandah that looked out towards the main square and at the rear were shower facilities. After a quick curry and lentil nosh, my first sit-down food in four days, I retired to my charpoy (rope bed). Amazingly in all the time since Delhi I hadn't seen a single Westerner. As I rolled out my sleeping bag my immediate neighbour engaged me in conversation. He was a local, likable, politely inquisitive and complementary about my dressing in local fashion. I was also going to try to learn the local dialect rather than lazily speak English. My greatest acquisition in this realm so far was the universal phrase 'Aja', loosely translated as 'O.K.' Being ex-Portuguese there is a Christian section of the population and some beautiful churches.

Initially I was surprised to learn that this native gentleman was a fervent adherent of the faith. This he expressed in a sweet and charming way—not at all pontifical or evangilising. What put the kibosh on me was when he asked my name—Christopher. I presume he assumed I was of his same beliefs. "Christo, Christo!" he exclaimed. We had been conversing in English but he obviously had an imperfect understanding of the language. He was insistent that he bring me a cup of tea in the morning at five o' clock. He would then accompany me to church mass which he would guide me to. He was so sweet about all this that I hadn't the heart to decline the offer. After agreeing to see him in the morning I bade him good night, lay down on my charpoy which felt heavenly and slept like a god.

True to his word tea arrived first thing. I felt relaxed and refreshed, then took a shower. However, I made it a reasonably quick one and whilst he was taking his I rolled up my bag and sneaked out of the hotel, which had been paid in advance, feeling like a criminal. It was the best I could do without openly hurting his feelings. I shrugged my shoulders. It might have been a cowardly way of doing things but I felt it diplomatic.

I made my way to the square. Many of the buildings here were whitewashed one or two-storey with good roofs and decently built. I had become accustomed to seeing Sanskrit and English signs and inscriptions, now there was also Portuguese and the local dialect. Several phrases that I had picked up the previous evening I forgot as quickly as I had learned. I was headed out for the beach area. I had absolutely no idea of the geography but got on a local bus that I believed was going where I wanted.

Boarding the bus for the first time it was not packed out which was a pleasant change. There was a more relaxed and slower pace. A lot of the women wore beautifully coloured saris, had immaculate complexions and long shining strong black hair. The bus really was local and seemed to meander around endlessly through the countryside. I hadn't eaten that day so as we slowed to a halt somewhere I took advantage of my immediate surroundings. There were huge broad leaves of banana trees overhanging the road. These came practically inside. All I had to do was reach out my arm and I was able to pick a large bunch of bananas.

I nodded off for a while not believing how long this journey was taking or having a clue where I was. Sometime in the afternoon the bus drew up under a canopy of palm-trees at a gathering of large russet covered low huts. Typical beach-huts in fact. I got off and looked around. On enquiring I was pointed to an establishment across the way larger that the rest. After negotiating several scrawny noisy wild dogs I made my way over and found it to be a communal resting place where beds were filed in one big open room. I took a bed and sat down. I needed to rest and thought to do so for a while before having something to eat and getting my bearings. Famous last thoughts. I asked someone what the time was—six o' clock. I lay back. I had come a long way.

When I opened my eyes again it was broad daylight. I was the only one in the room. On getting up to get some tea I found out it was midday. I had slept eighteen hours solid. Someone came in. The first Westerner I had seen. He was German and had been in the area a couple of years. He gave me some tips. One was avoid drinking milkshakes (of which there were several bars) from a medical point of view. Another was don't sleep on the beach at night away from a fire. It crawls with cobras which come out from the undergrowth.

Last night in fact someone had been bitten. If this does ever happen the thing to do is get hold of the snake pressing the nape of the neck and throat between fingers and thumb in order to keep its jaws forced open and take it to a doctor who can administer an antidote. Unfortunately the person bitten had done this but grabbed the snake around the neck so that they were bitten again several times on the way to the doctor. Very shortly after arriving they were stone-dead.

My location was near the well-known Anjuna beach so I set off for a walk. There was white sand lined with palm-trees in either direction. The waves of the Arabian sea flopped down and I paddled up to my ankles barefoot. Not a cloud in the sky and brilliant hot sun.

One thing I decided for myself, however tempting, was not to swim. I figured this from general knowledge of tropical waters and the aquatic life therein. These were not known shark waters it was true but there are other things; electric rays and giant jellyfish. This might have seemed like paranoia. There were a few people nude bathing right then. In a short distance I spotted, even from the shallows, a sea snake. These are lethal and move like greased lightening. I had made the right decision.

I walked for a mile or so then made my way back. Along the beach could be seen the remnants of the previous night's camp fires where parties had been held. I didn't want to stay in the same place that night so on enquiring around I managed to rent myself a smallish beach hut, with bed. This was basic but dirt cheap. There was no light so I invested in an oil-lamp.

Here I stayed for a week or so. There was plenty of night-life although the music left something to be desired. Every day was hot and sunny with the sea keeping it from being too much so. It was time for a bit of exploring away from this popular area. To go anywhere else one needs to go back to Panjim and out again which is what I did. Instead of taking a bus I found out you could hire a motorbike. I did and off I went wherever the fancy took me. No helmet or licence and a tank full of gas. I had a whole day bombing about which was great after being on a beach over a week.

My next move was to relocate so after a night in my old hotel I set off on another local bus picked completely at random. I was in another element now. Instead of pursuing a set destination I was indulging in pure wanderlust which I revelled in. This time the route went inland through a more cultivated area, open fields of rice in between the palm-trees with the occasional bent figure working.

The trip was purely rural stopping in the middle of nowhere to return whence we came so I got off. There had been hardly any passengers getting on or off. As the bus pulled away into the distance I was left standing in an almost eerie dusty hot silence I know not where. For the first time I had a strange attack of insecurity. There was not a soul in sight anywhere and no recognisable habitation. A momentary sense of directionless isolation hit me, welling up inside as if I was falling into a hole stripping me of feeling.

The sun beating down brought me to. Rather, would have passed me out if I had not moved from under it. I went to the shade of the nearest roadside tree. As I rested back on my rucksack I then spotted what I thought a truly extraordinary sight. A sign hanging up outside a palm-hut, which had not been visible from where I had previously been standing, displayed the coloured emblem of a kingfisher.

On closer inspection this turned out to be an advert for the main stock in trade at this establishment, namely bottled beer. I couldn't believe it, I had chanced on an Oriental pub. What the hell I thought. In I went and was the sole customer amidst a few scattered tables and chairs. The proprietor was a most genial man. The beer was like English light-ale and very good. I sat in the shade having a couple of these and felt a new man.

By now I was under the smug impression that I had mastered some local speech. The variations here are manifold. After a friendly experiment in this field with my host I bid him adieu. Where or when his next customer was to come from heaven only knew. I thought I had gathered from him that there was a bus departure every couple of hours. This must surely have been days, weeks or years. I gave up waiting and started to walk. Despite the heat I was glad to do this. Essentially the only true way to see anywhere, I covered a number of miles and to my surprise found I was near to a part of the coast further north from where I had been staying.

The track petered out to nothing, I passed through a grove of palm-trees and found myself on a completely virgin stretch of beach. There were fallen coconuts scattered here and there. Not having any implement I resorted to brute force in smashing one open on the base of a tree. This was successful providing a good drink.

In many ways I had spent a solitary day and in these unspoilt surroundings of pristine sand, warmth, shimmering palms, blue sea and sky I found myself becoming deeply reflective. I was on my own in a kind of private paradise. I didn't tangibly formulate my thoughts or feelings but just let them drift through me. I sat quietly for a while then meandered slowly by the water's edge. A little way along there was a small inlet of fresh-water to the sea. This was no more than three foot deep and about twelve wide. The water was crystal clear. In it shoals of tropical fish the like of which I had never seen flashed and moved in all directions. The colourings were spectacular and held me entranced. On the other side of the inlet the land rose up to a wood-covered cliff. I turned back and at the place I had arrived went to the water's edge staring out to sea for some time.

Retracing my steps, literally as mine were the only ones human or animal in the sand, I came back through the palm-grove and rediscovered the track. I wasn't actually sure this was the way I had come. There were no real landmarks but it seemed unfamiliar. In due course a largish solitary shack came into view and some savoury aromas hit my nostrils. A roadhouse no less.

As I came nearer I found this not the case. It was isolated in the middle of several fields. I had to leave the track and walk down the side of several irrigation channels to reach it. It was however, as some form of gastronomic sixth sense had hinted, a food-house, used I guessed mainly by workers from the fields. I went in without any of the several inhabitants batting an eyelid and was confronted by the sight and smells of good-looking curry.

I felt I was leading a somewhat charmed existence. Very courteously I was shown to a table and brought a beaker and jug of water. This I did not drink. In no time I was brought a huge dish of steaming hot rice, curry that was out of this world and a pile of chappatis for the princely sum of fifteen paise. There were one hundred paise to the rupee. A rupee was equivalent to seven pence sterling. My maths told me this was approximately one pence.

There was one minor drawback. Humans were not the only customers. Flies so dense in number they constituted a black veil settled on any food in sight. I was famished and intended to brave it. Swat, swat with the back of my hand. Up rose the offenders; to my chagrin within a second settling back down again.

I wasn't sure what to do. In a comical and probably suicidal course of action I adopted a method of swatting with one hand and scooping food with another in which exhaustive way I downed the lot. I blotted my mind from the hygiene aspect convincing myself the hot spices (for hot they were) would kill anything off (myself no-doubt being the most likely candidate). At the conclusion of this I sat back and felt most satisfied. As I gazed out of a side opening onto the green rice fields I felt truly in Asia.

I nudged myself out of a day-dream and departed. I was beginning to feel part of the general scene and not so wonderstruck. On a more practical note where was I staying tonight? Without being too bothered I just headed off down the road and as is often the case when you're not really wanting one a bus came trundling along. I stuck out a hand and off I was again.

In this part of Goa the buses headed for Panjim. I was becoming well-known at the hotel and on friendly terms with several people there. They were most hospitable. Amongst other aspects that appealed was the laid back timeless atmosphere. I stayed just one night again and thought to venture further north next day. There is virtually no railway in Goa, this system in India being due to the British. There is a line out further south at Marmagao. If it were possible bus travel was even cheaper so it was fine by me apart from the fact that with all the bumping and clanking about coupled with the climate I was becoming somewhat on the slim side.

The language was definitely improving so it was with some confidence I set off for the area I had in mind. This was born out by the shift in landscape. Rice fields began to be replaced by undulating land that had fruit and spice crops and then became even hillier. It was late morning when a stop was made to pick up a large number of passengers. This took some time whilst loose change was sorted. Presumably the people had walked from a distant village to this roadside stop in the country to go to market as they were nearly all loaded with various goods. Whilst this was going on I had leisure to take in the outside scene.

There was a very bright glare to everything from the sun. I suddenly got a sinister feeling. Something dark seemed to catch my attention from the corner of my eye. I looked more intently and there as the road sloped off the side down into a shallow verge not more than six feet from the vehicle was a long dark shape—that moved! Nearly as long as the bus, about thirty feet, was a python. I got a shudder and couldn't wait for the bus to move. When it did I felt a shiver pass over me and I wiped a few beads of perspiration from my brow.

The end of this route was at the crossing of a very wide river. There was a large ferry boat here but the bus did not go on to it. I boarded as a foot passenger. The river must have been a mile wide at this crossing, the water ran swirling and strong. As I leaned on the side admiring the view and enjoying the fresh breeze a voice spoke in my ear. I turned to see a man dressed like myself and with long blond hair and a goaty beard. He had spoken English but turned out to be German. After introductions he asked how long I had been here. He had been in Goa four years. As at this present time I had no idea where I was he offered to show me around a bit. This I happily accepted. We got on well.

I liked the fact that although he was obviously intelligent and knowledgeable he was also laid back and had a good sense of humour. It was pleasant to be in someone else's company after being on my own for a while. He certainly knew the terrain like the back of his hand and spoke the local language fluently. I felt almost lazy in that temporarily I didn't have the responsibility of decision making. A walk from the other bank of the river of a mile or so brought us to another crossing. This must have been a form of delta area. There was no steam ferry this time. For a small price you could cross in a canoe paddled by the owner.

The canoe was a sound but ancient-looking craft. As we pushed out of the reeds into the main stream the level of the sides was only a few inches above the current. My heart skipped a couple of beats as I knew there to be crocodiles in these parts. However our progress was steady. Once out in midstream I felt almost Amazonian or something akin to Livingstone and Stanley. I had a chuckle at this but the sensation of having the power of a huge flowing cross-current under your backside on only a thin strip of wood is unnervingly exciting. One tumble at that point would be your chops. The light was breathtaking as the sun was lowering, shining through the palms on the opposite shore and reflecting back off the water.

Safely on the other side and with night approaching shelter had to be sought. Carried by a cord on his shoulder my new friend had a very fine-looking flute. He explained to me it was his source of livelihood. He would go up into the surrounding hills of the villages and play. He had become known as Krishna and would obtain food and shelter. From now on I called him Krish. Krish and Chris. We laughed at this.

So this was our immediate course of action. I felt dubious but put myself in his hands as I was game and had nothing to lose. We wandered off into the undergrowth amid coconut-trees and up a small incline into a clearing. This was about a couple of miles. If Krish had deserted me I would have been well and truly lost as there were no landmarks at all. He was completely aware of his surroundings. He then sat down and started to play. It was very good. A dreamlike situation. The sound of flute floating in the warm evening air as the sun sank behind the jungle canopy.

After half an hour or so he stopped and descended down a slope. There appeared out of nowhere the roofs of huts made from interwoven palm-leaves which are large, broad and very resilient when dried out. Sure enough as Krish had said we were made welcome. All the people knew him, we were given food and a resting place for the night. Off we went next morning. We came near to the coast again.

I was introduced to a family in a fishing village we came to. The homes here were more substantial, although some were of the basic woven palm-leaf construction others were of Portuguese origin, larger with red brick or tiling made smooth in places for flooring. This family were very friendly and had a spare room in what amounted to their bungalow. I decided to stay here. We agreed on this. Krish was going to show me the local market then go on his way and I would return for evening meal. It was all highly satisfactory.

The market concerned was busy when we arrived. It was intimate with a covered central area containing many stalls and several in the surrounding square. The variety of fruit, spices, clothing, ornaments, scents, vegetables and goods of many kinds was a spectacle. I have always enjoyed browsing at places like this and I could see myself spending hours doing so here. Goats, cows and monkeys roamed all over to add to the picturesque scene. I also noticed several Westerners amongst the populace and was informed by Krish that this was a centre for trading that they came to. It was also at this point that we parted company. A brief but rewarding acquaintance.

I wandered round the market for the rest of the afternoon and then started to make my way back to my new abode. Initially breezing along in good spirits it suddenly occurred to me that I was now minus the navigational skills of Krish and I was blessed if I knew the way. We hadn't come by any recognisable track or path and had not gone through any other places in which to check or ask the way. I was relying on sense of direction and guesswork. As time passed I seemed to be getting nowhere fast. The same lush vegetation and thickly overhanging trees. Towards the coast undergrowth invariably thins out but if anything it was becoming denser, the going getting more difficult and I was entering real jungle. A sense of futility and helplessness began to pervade me.

Then, as the light began to fade panic set in. In the tropics the time-span between daylight and darkness is alarmingly short. There is not the lingering dusk of Europe. The implication of this fact hit me. I had no torch or light of any kind. I was lost in thick jungle wearing only plimsolls and it would soon be crawling with deadly snakes and God knows what. It wasn't fear that struck as I stumbled hurriedly on panting heavily, perspiration pouring off me—it was blind terror, as sure enough within no more than five minutes it was pitch-black.

Even the dark here seemed more intense. I could not see my hand in front of my face. I truly thought that I might well be for it in this situation. Just at this very point what I regarded as the appearance of a guardian angel: ping; ping; ping, ping, one by one small bright lights appeared before me dancing in the air. They were fireflies. Perhaps two dozen or so of them. They looked like something out of a fairy-tale. The light they emitted was quite brilliant having the luminosity of a sparkler on Guy Fawkes. This was enough to show the ground in front of me.

Instinct told me to just follow them as they danced through the air at walking pace. To culminate what I will always believe as a personal miracle, however much it could be explained away by fate or luck, these fireflies led me on until their light was interspersed with another larger, deeper glow, which as I neared I could make out to be the light from a hurricane-lamp. This was suspended from the veranda roof of a roadside house where I could now hear voices and see men playing cards outside.

Never in all my life had I been so relieved as I stumbled out of the jungle onto the track and up to the house. The expression on the men's faces was also a picture as I must have looked quite a sight appearing out of the dark wilderness in a petrified and bedraggled state.

The following day, having stayed the night at the road-house, I managed to negotiate my way back to the village. It was mid-morning when I arrived and the family I was to be staying with showed a touching concern for me. My room had been prepared for me. There was a nice bed, some simple furniture and some flowers had been placed around for decoration. It was also quite spacious. It was really beautiful and I felt at home straightaway. There were five members of the family; the parents, a daughter in her early teens and two sisters not yet of school age. They all had unpronounceable names.

Being a fishing village sometime that day whilst talking to Dev (my shortened name for the man of the house) the idea came up of me going out with the men the following day. In the week I lived in my tiny hut near Anjuna I had sampled some freshly cooked fish one morning. It was not a serious activity there being more of a holiday beach. Here it was the main livelihood. The fish itself was delicious and cheap. It was very good food to have, high in protein, no fat used as it was grilled and totally fresh. The majority of the catch after being sorted and boxed is sent to market. All the fishermen retain a quantity for domestic consumption and share in the price from the market, not only the local market but many places inland also.

The next morning as the sun rose I was given a call and off we went. The method most commonly used here was trawling—manual trawling. What happened was all the men from the village, about three dozen, assembled on the beach, then spread out and took hold of a vast length of netting. This was bunched up and you could carry it either under one or two arms at waist level. Everyone then waded out to sea.

My previous fears of hazardous aquatic life-form being allayed by Dev who assured me any serious incidents were rare. As he had been doing this all his life I bowed to his experience, privately still retaining doubts. The increase in depth of water is very gradual. It was not until we were approximately quarter of a mile out that we stopped. We had to be still and wait for what was considered a propitious moment. This was inborn through sharp eyes and generations of practice.

The waters here are certainly rich in life. Shoals upon shoals would come between us and the beach. The netting had large bulbous weights attached to the bottom end. The men were arranged in an ark. We then dropped the net down and trawled it back inland. This was simplicity itself. The exercise was repeated several times and the catch was plentiful. Then the sorting took place by a handful of selected men. I continued to take part everyday of my stay here and had fresh grilled fish every morning. It was a great way of life. I was up with the rising sun, plenty of sea water and exercise all combined to make me feel healthy.

The women were constantly mending the nets and a few men had boats in which they went further out to sea. The life was a rural one and the people were mostly happy and friendly. I did pick up common local phrases but was asked to speak English as Dev wanted his children to learn this. In fact I used to spend a couple of hours each evening teaching all three girls to write. They were very bright and quick to learn.

Although I had not expected anything in return, as I found it a pleasure, this was taken into consideration with the arrangement I had. For going fishing every morning, helping with any incidental heavy work and teaching most evenings I had no charge for my accommodation, ate my meals with the family and actually received fifty rupees a week from the fishing syndicate. The added beauty of all this was that I had the days free as well. I was in clover.

I made a trip inland to see if there was any mail for me post restante and to send some. Outside the main Post Office there was a bed of cacti in spectacular flower. I took this opportunity to wander round some of the back streets of Panjim and visit the old town of Goa. On my walk I came across a wholesale warehouse that specialised in exporting cashew nuts. They were more common than sand here. I also happened on the church where the relics of St Francis Xavier were reputed to be contained.

Out of interest I made enquiries and was shown the said antiquities. It did give me a sense of history. The saint was said to have visited here in the fifteen forties. He then went onto Japan and China where he died. How his relics came to be in Goa or as the their authenticity I do not know. The airport here is named after the explorer Vasco Da Gama who died further south at Cochin in fifteen twenty-four.

On my return to the village things went on as before and time passed without my noticing it. The brief visit to the outside world had sown a seed in me though. I began to feel a desire for further horizons. Having spoken to Dev with this in view I made my way south to Marmagao.

AND BACK

I. THE THIRD RIPPLE

ARRIVING IN THE AFTERNOON in the small town it seemed to be a particularly hot day. Probably because of my absence from crowds for a long time I found the noise and bustle intense. The town is not much further south but doesn't have the same ex-colonial feel as the rest of Goa and there appeared to be a higher population. I located the train. There was no station, just a literal end of the line halt. Standing there was a magnificent steaming and panting engine looking like some dark monster from a prehistoric world of iron beasts.

Departure wasn't due for a couple of hours so I explored the market. It was mainly fruit and vegetables so by way of diversion I approached a street seller who carried a tray-shaped board in front of his waist and hung by a strap round his neck. It reminded me of the ladies who sold icecreams during the intermission in the cinema of my childhood.

On this particular tray though were combustible items and appurtenances therewith. Chiefly catching my eye was a selection of small interestingly coloured cone-shaped packets. These contained bedis—miniature cigarettes. There are about twelve to a cone. They are khaki green, non-filtered and hardly the price of a box of matches. Essentially they are small leaves of tobacco rolled and gummed. I was not a regular smoker but had indulged occasionally. These were something else. Strong had nothing on it. It was not an experience I intended to repeat. I sat down in the shade and waited for the train to leave.

I had not formulated any kind of plan and there was no obvious place to purchase a ticket. The usual stirring and commotion arose intimating imminent departure. What I hadn't bargained for was the accommodation situation—namely, none. Seemingly the whole population of the town and all of Goa with it was making a mass exodus on this one, not very large, train. Apparently the frequency of the service is limited. I had been milling around without success when the carriages started to move.

Everywhere was full, all the corridors and entrances were blocked. Virtually the entire length of the train was taken up by what I termed outside 'hangers'. There was only one thing for it. Without thinking, I clambered on to some protrudence at the end of one of the carriages and struggled up, with the aid of an outstretched hand from a precursor, onto the roof. Here I joined a not insignificant band of kindred spirits. Before I had known what was happening I was squatting down amongst a conclave of roof-travellers and speeding out into the Indian countryside.

This mode of travel was a little unnerving at first. The fact that those around me took it as a matter of course helped reassure me. After a while the tables were turned and my nerves of apprehension became ones of exhilaration. I had no idea where I was headed, the air wafted onto my face and through my clothes and sunlight poured down on the foliage of wayside trees. I had a feeling of almost reckless freedom. If there was an element of irresponsibility I rejoiced in it. I had not one care in the world and felt I was about to do some real travelling.

One might imagine that sleeping would not be an agreeable matter in the circumstances. On the contrary. The rhythmic motion of the train and the facility to stretch out in the balmy night air combined to give me a fine slumber. There is an unspoken comradeship whereby anyone is prevented from getting too near the edge by whoever is awake at the time—fortunately, perhaps through instinct, someone always is.

The morning found me in mountainous forest in the heart of the South. I found out that it would not be long before we reached the city of Bangalore. When we arrived I did not intend to stay long as I had now got the urge to move. I did take the opportunity to look around the main streets though. It was fascinating to see several incense export-houses. Having seen the name of Bangalore on the side of so many boxes in England when it conjured up visions of far away exotic places and here I was strolling along. The climate here was pleasant as it was high up and dry. However in a matter of hours I was on my way again.

Most of the travellers 'abandon ship' before entering a main station as the train slows. The same applies in reverse to departure. I had plumped for a ticket this time—by way of variation as much as anything else. I was headed south again, my general idea being to get to the uttermost tip eventually at Cape Comorin and to see as much as possible in the process. By this stage I rather stupidly began to see myself as a bit of a seasoned traveller. Nethertheless I did strike up several conversations with local people who were interested to learn of other parts they had no real knowledge of. In this way journeying passed quickly and enjoyably. In spite of, or as experience taught me because of, the fact I was travelling alone I was never lonely. Given the capricious nature this adventure was taking I could have been a nightmare to accompany anyway.

Late the following day I was back on the coast, albeit further south, in the southernmost state of Kerala. The final stop was Trivandrum where I planned to down tools for a while. The train had gone north for some distance on its way to Mangalore, a busy trading seaport. This was the last stop before doubling back on the same route. It followed the coastline closely for some way giving a balmy air to the journey. All this time the scenery seemed to becoming even richer.

There is intense rainfall during the monsoon and I knew I was deep in the Tropics, the daily temperature never being less than around eighty degrees. There was a halt at Calicut which I spent some time exploring. This was where Vaco Da Gama first landed in India. It also gave its name to calico cloth. I obtained a printed scarf of the material here, which was useful as shade as opposed to keeping me warm. On the move again the track went inland before returning near the coast for the final stretch passing through Kasaragod, Cannamore, Tellicherry, Mahé, Badagara and thence Trivandrum, journey's end.

I found a small guest-house and spent the next day unwinding. There was a calm atmosphere pervading the place, it was small without being cramped and felt fresh and clean. It was a welcome respite from hot and dusty days on the move. I even went to the extraordinary lengths of washing my clothes, which dried in no time in the small courtyard which was decked out with large pots and urns full of luxuriant cacti and plants. On making my first recognisance of the town I noticed how frequently and with what clear diction English was spoken. There are many temples here which are works of art in themselves. The multilayered intricate handcarvings of figures and deities of every description have a bewildering effect. There is a dedicated craft of carving that takes many years of apprenticeship.

There are also many cottage industries connected with the coconut-palm. A different world from that of mass production. Whether one is an adherent or not I don't think the other-world effect of entering one of these temples can be denied. They hold a fascination that a lifetime could be spent exploring. To fulfil my plan to look out to the Indian Ocean I had to take a local bus to Kolachel and thence to Nagercoil. It was then a question of legging it to the Cape. It was yet another of the endless warm days with a clear blue sky when I did this. I stood still for some time in my solitary position at the tip the subcontinent.

As I was returning I saw a group of people building a bonfire whom I approached. They were suspicious at first but soon accepted me. They were having a party with food which I was invited to join. Part of the cuisinical itinerary I afterwards found out was python steak. I was glad I did not know before I ate it although it wasn't bad, something between herring and tuna only larger with little flavour. The complexion of the inhabitants here is charcoal and in the twilight with the flames blazing as it grew dark it was one of my more memorable moments. It seemed timeless.

After sleeping close to the fire that night I made my way back to Trivandrum. Whilst in this area I wanted to visit Cochin. It is commonly regarded as the earliest European settlement in India. There is an ancient Christian tradition in the area, first conversions being ascribed to the Apostle Thomas. I spent a day on a hired boat negotiating some of the maze of canals that link the coastal backwaters and lagoons which possess great beauty besides being useful as a means of transport. Like Goa there is extensive fishing here although with more use of boats with enormous nets for deeper water.

Further inland is a vast expanse of dense jungle in what is known as 'Silent Valley'. This is primeval forest and I had a yearning to do some exploring. My earlier experience made me think better of it though. I was told by a local that if you are out in the area at night there are giant leeches in the trees that can sense your body warmth and will drop on you by the score. That was enough for me.

The land beyond this rises to the Cardamom hills. I made a point of going there as the spice of the same name had always intrigued me. It is grown in great quantity and is highly aromatic. I found the experience naturally intoxicating as the views are also splendid without being overdramatic. The drier air in the hills is always a relief from the moist, sometimes steamy, climate lower down. Much of the area is given over to rubber, tea and coffee plantations.

It was time to move on. I had thought of going to Ceylon. I heard that you needed a certain amount of money on you to gain entrance. True of false my funds weren't exactly overflowing so I gave it a miss and started to make my way back north, initially making a relatively short journey of about a hundred and fifty miles to the city of Madurai. This is a great centre of Hinduism and the temple is one of the most famous in India. It has outstanding carvings both inside and out. Having spent a few hours there I had a choice of waiting some time for an express to Madras and onwards or getting a local stopper immediately. I went for the stopper.

Tiruchchiripalli, Kumbakonam, Nagappattinam, Chidambaram and Cuddalore were just some of the many places passed through. I then had to decide between stopping at Pondicherry and then perhaps going on to Madras or transferring to an all-nighter to Bangalore. There is a well known ashram at Pondicherry where lots of Westerners have congregated. I had seen one or two of them on my travels. Wearing a kind of uniformed orange-clothing and beaded medallion wasn't my cup of tea so on it was. Two days later found me back in Goa, exhausted but enriched with a head full of images and experience.

I made a mistake whilst hanging about for a bus back to the village. Blasé at having no particular health problems I sampled a milk-shake from the enticing range at a booth. They are moreish and I downed two or three. A couple of hours later, having rejoined Dev's family, I was making hurried sanitary visits. These persisted through the night and left me feeling drained. Eventually, being very tired, I slept until late next day.

After my coast to coast journeying a period of stability was required and for a while I settled back into a routine, fishing in the morning, writing during the day and teaching at night. Something told me this could not go on forever. Insidiously something physical began to tell me just that. Internal malfunction. These problems would vanish for a time and then recur with increased severity. It got to a stage where I sought medical advice. The news was not good. A form of dysentery was the diagnosis. It could resolve itself naturally or become more serious. I had come to another watershed. Although in many ways idyllic, if a tropical disease is contracted, the Tropics are for several reasons not the best place to be. In a period of respite I took the bull by the horns and departed. It was a wrench but I was guided by instinct.

II. EXIT STAGE LEFT

BY CHANCE I DISCOVERED it was possible to take a passenger ship from Goa to Bombay. This appealed to me and I booked a passage at the ticket office. This was a daily trip, the vessel was in dock and due to depart in an hour or so. It appeared a grand white steamer, old fashioned looking in some respects but very impressive. I was able to board straightaway. I got a thrill walking around the decks which were on three levels. When what was obviously the captain and fellow officers came on board up the gang plank in white shorts, socks and plimsolls wearing impressive naval caps looking very smart the naval scene was set.

Idiot that I am, I then indulged in another piece of lunacy. There was a refreshment bar on board. Something I had avoided all this time and said to myself I must sample before leaving, was some of the local wine. There is both rice and what I was told was either coconut or cashew. I purchased a bottle and then went and sat on the shady side of the deck to relax in the sea air. I was joined by a Westerner whose nationality I didn't find out and we spun each other some yarns. The refreshment was alright to begin with in a discusting sort of way. Several horn-blasts from the huge red funnels told us we were on our way and gracefully we slipped out of harbour.

It was a lovely sensation cruising along, the water being smooth. The coastline was constantly in sight giving a view of the palm-fringed beaches. The rice wine and motion of the ship had a combined undersirable effect on me making walking about a hazardous operation so when Bombay was finally reached I was glad to find my land legs again.

I bid farewell to my brief nautical companion and, unappealing as the prospect was, thought it best in the circumstances to stay overnight. I daresay if you're staying in a top-notch hotel the facilities would be fine. On my budget not so. The impact of the city on me was made greater by being in the country so long. It bombards with smell, dirt, noise, crowds and chaos—to me a nightmare. Not everyone feels like this of course as there is a hum of life and excitement especially at night. There are some very fine public buildings. I passed the Courts of Justice and Victoria Rail Station. They are splendid Walt Disney-looking places. The centre of the film industry is in Bombay. There was only one cinema in Goa that I saw. Here they are everywhere and patronised by crowds of enthusiasts.

Despite my forebodings I did manage to find a reasonable room in an area where every other shop seemed to be an astrologer's or fortune-teller's. They are great believers here and will even do certain things on certain days accordingly. All this was round the corner from the red-light district. It was humid and I didn't plan on being here long.

I was up early next morning. The tea I had didn't go down too well but before long I was on my way, leaving the metropolis behind. This was a long haul to Delhi so I sat back third-class and watched the world go by.

With the usual variety of occupants there was never a dull moment and I delighted in overhearing and sometimes joining in the constant chatter. Time passed quickly like this but come dusk I was tired. I did not fancy sleeping in a sitting position so necessity being the mother of invention I swung myself up onto the luggage-rack—to the amusement of several of my fellow passengers—stretched out and had a glorious rest.

Come dawn I was presented with a chai from someone below and told I had innocently escaped part of the fare as the inspector had thought I was luggage! The rest of the day went smoothly resulting in punctual arrival in Delhi.

From now on I was in uncharted territory, organisationally speaking. Train was definitely the best bet to Amritsar. There were dozens of coaches going that way, some on to Europe. I had enough of that mode of transport and it meant a bulk payment. It began to sink in that I wasn't exactly loaded, so the quicker I moved the better. Therefore without stopping in Delhi I was able in the early hours of the morning to make a connection for Amritsar which is the final stop on the Indian side before entering Pakistan. This had meant hanging around Delhi station for interminable hours and travelling all day again so when I reached my destination

I was exhausted. I found a small hotel, had a curry which tentatively settled, went to my room, flopped down on the bed and turned out the light. Not for long. Plop. I jumped up with a start and switched on the light. Something had fallen on my face. I looked up at the ceiling. I hadn't noticed before. It was covered in green lizards looking like a Maurits Escher print. They fell off in the dark so I had to sleep in the full glare all night.

It was hot in the morning and I was glad of a shower. Steam was rising off the recently washed courtyard as I ventured forth to work out my agenda. There wasn't a train until evening so I went back to the hotel and simply rested up in a wicker chair under a fan. It seemed cooler in the shade during the day. At night the fans just blow hot air around. It was a relaxed place with its venetian-style windows and small communal garden and I felt as if I needed the rest.

As evening approached it was time to make my way to the station. I ambled through the sultry streets walking out of India. Arriving at dusk I propped my rucksack against a wall, squatted down, leant back and waited. The station isn't huge but large enough to contain a constant hum of activity. I was absorbed in watching this when I was approached by two figures who looked like Old Testament prophets come down from the Mount. They had straggling beards, long robes and were carrying staffs. The weirdest thing of all was when they asked me if I spoke English. The last place in the world I would have thought or expected to hear under the circumstances—a broad Mancurian accent.

It turned out that part of my initial impression wasn't totally out of line with events. They were originally friends in Manchester, about a couple of years older than me, and had come out to Kashmir. They had been several months staying up in the mountains in a cabin but had recently been set on by bandits and robbed. They had come down from the mountains on foot, which had taken two weeks. The staffs were for protection against wolves and bears as they had been sleeping in the open. No wonder they looked haggard.

The initial reason for them approaching me was that they were unfamiliar with the rail system. Apart from that they were undecided as to what course of action to take, the bottom line being that they were penniless. One of them, Ian, was for flying a train to Delhi, going to the Embassy and trying for repatriation. The other, Rob, was for chancing their arm the other way, the way I was going, by begging, free-riding and trusting to luck.

Ian suggested that if their present luck continued they wouldn't get very far. They were certainly thin if not emaciated. Rob reckoned to get as near to England as possible and then when all else failed trying for repatriation as a last resort. I explained my situation and offered to pay their initial fare over the border, if that was the direction they decided on, as there is virtually no way of free-loading a border pass. The result of discussion was Ian going for Delhi and Rob joining up with me. They parted company and I went to get Rob his ticket while he minded my gear.

Small things can mean a lot in certain circumstances and I felt a sense of release and freedom not having to haul that stuff around with me and knowing it would be safe when I got back was also comforting. We spent the rest of the time awaiting our arrival by exchanging experiences. It felt strange to have a travelling companion again, especially an English one. Having for so long been associated with places, things and people foreign and learnt to speak local dialects it had a combined sense of out of placeness and reassurance to be with another whose language and terms of reference were synonymous with your own. In adversity an innate sense of unspoken mutual trust is formed.

As time passed the platform became more and more congested so we thought it prudent to move to the edge to improve our accommodation chances. This was easier said than done as without our realising it had insidiously become jammed solid. Employing rugby tactics we did manage to make some headway. When the train arrived there was pandemonium and despite our best efforts the most we could achieve was crushing into the outer corridor. Even this position looked in peril as due to some mysterious bodily swelling (those safe inside spreading out no doubt in their satisfaction) we were being pushed towards ejection.

There was no way I was missing this train. Desperate remedies for desperate situations. The toilet right next to the entrance, completely flooded out as we discovered due to the squatty hole being blocked, but nothing else for it and in we went up to our ankles. Standing was the only position short of near death so with the heat and stench this was the longest thirty-five mile journey I ever made.

There was no open window so it was difficult to breath even with the door wide open and I began to feel nauseous vomiting several times due to the noxious gaseous odour. To rub salt in the wound three times we had to produce our tickets. How the inspectors got through was an utter mystery. It was one of only a handful of times I had bought a ticket, a fine example of Sod's Law in reverse. If the great railway hierarchy had been aware of it no doubt they would have seen it as poetic justice. Whatever happens to someone without a ticket in these conditions I couldn't guess or for that matter what the authorities did in general about a practice that was so widespread it was a way of life. On route for the first time in ages I was asked to produce my passport. I had nearly forgotten I was abroad in a way being so used to moving freely around. This brought it back. The passport itself immediately became an object of veneration which I had to hand around individually for examination by those passengers closest to me.

Finally we reached Lahore and the nightmare was over. At least that's what I thought. The train we arrived on would be going back the way we came. To pursue our journey we had to catch what was in effect the connection of a shuttle service. The train onwards from Lahore would now be Pakistani, coming into the station and returning in the opposite direction as well.

All this took part on the same platform and involved engines changing ends. The station here is a large one as Lahore is a big city. Many passengers were doing the same thing as us so as a consequence a huge amount of people merely poured out of the train and onto the nearside of the platform not wanting to be away from the edge. There was already a vast number of people waiting when we pulled in. One way of describing the ensuing mayhem is to picture a human wave crashing on a beach.

After this had died down we found we were in for another longish wait. It was about eleven o' clock when we arrived and our connection finally pulled in around one. After our last experience I wasn't going in search of tickets so we just squatted down in a reasonable position whilst the nether regions of our attire dried off in the warm night air. It was a relief to be sitting down but the air was still oppressive and I'm sure that in many other circumstances the aroma that we must have been emitting would have served to cocoon us with a natural barrier several feet around us and parted the human tide wherever we went.

On this occasion it was not so. We were just as much sardines in a can as ever. One of the added reasons for this shortly became apparent. When the train arrived not that many people got off. This was perplexing at first. We found out later that, being in the know, people from further up the line had got on and stayed on, redoubling their journey to ensure seats.

All the information concerning the logistics of the journey was gleaned by a combination of various disjointed pieces of sign language, pidgeon English and a mixture of dialects as there was a wide ethnic diversity. I think I must have ended up speaking some new form of Oriental Esperanto combining Gujurati, Urdhu, Parsee, English and goodness knows what else. It would certainly make an interesting new branch of language. It served its purpose for us.

Those boarding in Lahore were fairly scuppered. Unbelievably the situation was far worse than Amritsar which I couldn't have imagined possible. At least you had a sporting chance there as when the train pulled in it then emptied. The route markers on the side of the carriages confirmed this to be the train we wanted. You could feel a sense of panic in the air. Rob and I looked at each other with telepathic despair in our eyes. After an initial surge forward and fruitless scramble we both intuitively went limp and both literally and metaphorically threw our hands up in the air. The time gap between departures is wide—a day even—maybe more, it appeared to be in the lap of the gods. And then to go over the whole procedure all over again. I conjured up a mental picture of Sisyphus forever pushing a rock up a hill only for it to roll down again. It didn't bear thinking about and I didn't want to grow old doing this.

Rail travel here is certainly no joke but I have to say I never once saw anyone lose their temper or get seriously agitated. This is part of the mystique of the Orient to a Westerner. Outwardly there is frantic chaos everywhere but it is all conducted with a confounding spirit of calm, good humour and passive acceptance. This can be both endearing and furiously irritating increased by mental oscillation deciding which between the two to adopt. Certainly a land of paradox.

However here we were, seemingly helpless and had, for the moment at least, apparently had it. We were going through the motions of discussing what we could do when out of nowhere a voice came to us; not an inner, but a real one. We both looked doubtingly around. It seemed to come from above the crowd and was distinguished by its clarity. Not far from us I caught sight of a lady's face.

"English, are you English?"

I looked up at her enquiringly and she repeated the question.

"Yes," I said and nodded.

"Quickly, quickly, in here."

She motioned into the half opened part of a carriage door where she was standing. Without questioning we made a bee-line for this. We climbed up the steps and were ushered inside by a more diminutive female standing in the shadow as the door was pushed quickly to behind us. The lady, who was quite tall, then beckoned us down a short passage and we duly followed. We then entered a spacious compartment and were proffered wide wicker chairs on which to be seated.

In a dreamlike sense of bewilderment we took these. The lady sat opposite us and the shorter of the two closed the door and remained standing by the side of it.

"My name is Lakshmi," she said. "I saw your predicament and heard your voices. What is your destination?"

"I'm Chris and this is Rob," I replied. "We are going to Peshawar and then on to England."

She was going to Islamabad just outside Rawalpindi which is about two-thirds of the way to Peshawar. The girl was her maid and we were welcome to share the compartment thus far. She did not like to see foreign travellers having a bad time of it in her country or wish them to form an unfavourable image.

We couldn't thank her enough. She was dressed elegantly and we became self-conscious of our state which must have showed. Without any embarrassment we were offered the use of the washroom which we accepted gratefully. Then we were asked if we were hungry which we answered in the affirmative. We carried on chatting and drinking tea. In a short time the maid came through from a separate catering section with a hot meal for us all which was delicious. By this time Rob was on his last legs and was asked if he wanted to rest. He had an overhead couchette prepared for him in the maid's section and was soon out like a light.

I seemed to have got a second wind and besides my hostess appeared keen to carry on the conversation, showing no inclination to retire to her own quarters. She had in fact been a student at Oxford and was keen to hear news about England, general events and politics. She was also interested in my goings on and my impression of the country. We talked for hours. Eventually she withdrew and I curled up on a couch. It was the most gracious hospitality indeed.

The next morning found us on the outskirts of Rawalpindi. The surrounding countryside looked refreshed and clean. There had obviously been some recent rain as in places steam was rising from the remains of wayside puddles. The early morning sun was gleaming on the foliage everywhere and against a clear blue sky it was all strikingly green. I even got sight of an immaculately cut cricket ground, looking as smooth as a billiard table, complete with pavilion. All this in contrast to the recent dust and heat of India gave it the look and feel of a summer's morning in England.

Our host began to make preparations for disembarkation and we deemed it appropriate to make our adieus, once more expressing our truly heartfelt gratitude. The connection in Rawalpindi was straightforward and the congestion had eased considerably. We were able to get seats and the hundred miles or so to Peshawar passed smoothly.

After recent events I felt a sense of relief and drifted into a tranquil daydream.

On nearing our destination we felt the need to stretch our legs and went to stand at a carriage exit. It was getting hot so it was fun to stand on the edge with the wind rushing through your hair. We were joined by several local men. I wasn't sure what they ate in this part of the world but we were dwarfed by them. I was glad they were of an amiable disposition. This was characteristic of virtually everywhere I had been.

Peshawar was journey's end at this point in time because although there is an extension of the line to Landi Kotal for some unknown reason it was not operational at present. Obtaining directions for a hotel, it turned out to be the same one I had stayed in on my way through before. It was reasonably priced and a popular place for travellers of our ilk. We went up the two flights of stairs to our room shared with three other occupants and took time out.

After a brief rest I woke to a cacophony of metallic clattering. This I discovered was coming from a mechanics' yard adjacent to the hotel. The Oriental version of siesta didn't seem to apply here. I was covered in perspiration and it really was stiflingly hot with an air of deep humidity and yet as I looked out of the window there were a dozen or so men and boys beavering about, banging and clanking, most of them not even in the shade. It transpired that a lot of in-transit repair work was done here for passing coaches and vans; an Eastern pit-stop.

Nor did it look as if the workers weren't feeling the heat, the perspiration was pouring off them.

No wonder they looked thin. Apart from the gate entrance the yard itself was completely enclosed by a high wall creating an oven and I noticed most of the mens' hands were wrapped in bandages to enable them to handle metal. The reason for them being active at this time was that it was in fact the hotel compound. Everything was dormant when we arrived but now activity was in full flow because at night the hotel would fill up. I went downstairs to explore.

The reception area was a multi-purpose space. Leading out from it were tables and chairs where you could eat, have a drink or just sit. It was a communal meeting and hanging out place. Music was played on a stereo. There was a large notice-board where personal messages could be left and travel information obtained.

The reason for the hotel filling up at the moment was that there had been a landslide in the Khyber Pass so travel was suspended. Not exactly 'Casablanca' but we were stuck here for the present. I got myself a tea and took a seat. Whether it was me or not I don't know but there seemed to be an insular atmosphere, almost cliquey amongst the exclusively Western clientele and whilst not being blatantly stand-offish certainly weren't overtly forthcoming.

I thought this ironic considering they were all foreigners and virtually everywhere I had been where I was the only foreigner the locals had generally been very friendly. There was a kind of feeling of everyone or small group doing there own thing and ne'er the twain shall meet. This may have been coming from some of those who were on their way eastwards and that they still had a subconscious feeling of superiority which experience rubs out. Perhaps it was just that it was hot and humid.

The banging from outside had now ceased but it was no exaggeration to say that the heat was like a sauna and this in itself can cause tension. Not feeling like eating I went upstairs to lay on my bed. I was restless. The heat was getting to me. In an attempt to divert my thoughts I tried reading a book I came across left on a bedside table. A more incongruous book for the circumstances I would find it hard to imagine—Perry Mason. I found it impossible to concentrate though and gave up.

After spending a fitful night tossing and turning the morning brought no relief in the weather. I went down to the desk thinking I ought to try some food. The menu catered for Europeans but I was informed that none of the various items containing eggs were available, that because it was so hot they were virtually cooking in their shells. This was in all seriousness.

The temperatures were at record levels even for this area which can notoriously have extreme variations. Today it was one hundred and forty degrees Fahrenheit in the shade! I checked that this was forty and not fourteen. I then found out that the Pass was still closed so there was nothing for it but to have some tea and retire again. In these conditions I found my head starting to swim. There was no air at all so thinking to cool off I went for a cold shower.

Thankfully it did actually work but conditions were such that the water was coming out warm. The only thing I could find to do in complete lethargy was to sit down on the tiled floor and just let the shower pour over me. Unbelievably I did this for several hours. It was the only way to keep cool. Eventually I came out looking like a shrivelled walnut.

The mechanics were at it again in the yard, some welding with blow-torches. A marvel how they coped. Still unable to settle I ventured out to a shaded part of the courtyard. On striking up a conversation with a young assistant it transpired he owned a motorbike and would I like a ride round the outskirts of the city? I was all for it. Anything to escape being slowly cooked in this oven. So on the back and whoosh—off we went.

What a relief to have a wind. I didn't take in much of the surroundings, just glad to be mobile for an hour. On returning the news was that the Pass was open and transport would resume in the morning. Rob and I had been doing our own thing but now had a mini-conference. Funds were becoming low so we decided on getting a local bus to the border on the morrow. Somehow I regained an appetite that evening, was in better spirits and slept well.

In fact we managed to secure seats through to Kabul at very reasonable prices. This was one of the buses that are fantastically decorated and packed inside with passengers. The roofs are piled high with luggage so what suspension there is undergoes a real work-out. The spacing between the seats is narrow so all in all there are more comfortable ways to travel. The main thing was it was getting us there.

Inside, the fascinating aspect about the exclusively male local speech was that it varied without a moment's notice from an almost deafening row of excited interchange to a hushed silence with corresponding alteration of facial expression from animated exclaim to a calm look of remote aloofness.

When we arrived at the border there was a back-log because of the closure so there was a delay getting through. Once again there was a plethora of heavily armed tribesmen in evidence, many on horseback. With the disused fort in the background and the surrounding barren rocky scenery there is no escaping the medieval feel of this place with all its historical military associations of invasion, incursion and repulsion.

The wait wasn't too bad, presumably because the pass was clear in both directions and there had been a period of interia at the border posts. We were now bound 'up the Khyber'. The journey up is no less hair-raising than coming down. The main difference is of course in speed.

On stretches the bus really crawls. Then the possibility of stalling and the hazardous consequences this could entail spring up to enliven the mind. The site of the recent slide was passed. Despite most of the rubble having been cleared you could see that if there had been any traffic at the time it would have been goodbye.

Due to the slow pace the ascent obviously takes a lot longer but gradually as our altitude rose the oppressive heat of the plain began to recede, which was indeed an immense relief, literally coming up for air. However it was still hot and at one of the rare places where it is possible to stop we did so, for what actual purpose I was not sure. Everyone got off to stretch. I went further than this. We were at a spot where the road was virtually level with the downcoming Kabul river. It was a gushing torrent just here but at the edge the flow was not so powerful. One or two Westerners on the bus had come down near me to splash their faces.

To their amazement, and really to mine, on impulse I went right in completely submerged with the roar of the current rushing through my hair and over my body. I then drank in several long draughts of the icy liquid figuring it would be clean. Reckless it might have been, wonderful it was. I stood up waist high in surging cold mountain water as it cascaded over the shining rocks bubbling and foaming all around me.

It was an elemental feeling with bright sun overhead shining out of a clear deep-blue sky illuminated and sparkling on the water breakers, framed on both sides by sheer craggy cliffs which cast long dark chilling shadows. I had a conscious sense of time suddenly standing still and I was quite alone, alive and in the middle of a mountain range in central Asia.

Voices brought me back to my immediate surroundings. If I stayed where I was any longer I really would have been on my own. The shouts were to tell me the bus was about to go. I hurriedly clambered out and back on board. The locals no doubt thought us foreign travellers mad. This merely confirmed it. It was an experience I wouldn't have missed for worlds. A glimpse of natural freedom where for me time had ceased.

Through Jalalabad and back in Kabul again, staying in Chicken Street. The mysteries of the Orient; there is no on-going transport at present so a few days stay here at least are envisaged. We are in a dormitory-room with an interesting cross-section of inhabitants. A Frenchman who smokes a lot. As time here can stretch out this is an occupation indulged in by many.

My immediate neighbour and I unfortunately have something in common, we are both beginning to suffer 'Montezuma's Revenge'. He has a penchant for carrot juice, labouring under the misguided belief that as this is naturally free from fats and water it will do him good. It's the eye of a needle job. He is up and down from his bed to make visits outside more often that I am. There is no warning with this either which is disconcerting. This went on all day and night. The result is exhausting, keeping no nutrition inside and generally debilitating. Being virtually bedstricken there is the tedium as well.

It turned out that this was not all we had in common. Whilst we lay there we passed the time as best we could in conversation and got on very wellsharing an ironic sense of humour in our fate. He was a German by the name of Heinrich. Before coming out this way he had been staying in London. Oh really I said, what part? Harrow-on-the-Hill. The old hackneyed phrase 'it's a small world'. This was where I was born.

After a couple of days performing the 'Aztec two-step' things seemed to ease a bit so I decided to venture out. Rob had no problems. As it was mid-afternoon there were not many people about. I was accosted on a corner by a young urchin trying to interest me in what looked liked ancient chocolate bars at just a few Afghanis—very cheap. My suspicions lay elsewhere as to the nature of the produce. I wandered into a second-hand book shop and picked up a copy of Gormanghast.

There was a jeweller's nearby and though I couldn't really afford it I bought a reasonably priced chunky ring. It was nice to be strolling along. I noticed the air here was thinner due to the increased altitude. I could hear myself breath slowly as I walked. Probably also due to my recent bout I felt light-headed. I carried on for some way finding myself entering a comfortable-looking residential area. In the distance the purple folds of the Koh-i-Baba Mountains came into view.

Later that evening seated in a wicker chair on the veranda of the enclosed hotel garden in the cool night air I decided to have a go at a salad—with success. Emboldened by this I made a foray to the extremely colourful bazaar next evening. There was a wonderful variety of food-stuffs on display.

I was side-tracked on my way back. A casual passing word resulted in me sitting clandestinely behind closed doors in front of a modern wonder—a refrigerator, out of which was produced, on condition of a vow of silence and five pounds sterling, a can of beer. Insane to part with that cash—but what a drink.

Five days in Kabul and finally there was a bus. Just as well as my money was fast running out. It was an Afghan bus to Kandahar. The usual conditions as we set off mid-morning—only accompanied towards the back inside by about two dozen live chickens in baskets and a free roaming goat. Never a dull moment. As the day wore on and we headed south the heat increased and the atmosphere inside was something. The goat probably thought we stank more than him. We had been non-stop into the night when we had a welcome rest. In the middle of nowhere was a solitary chai-dwelling. A fire was made outside and everyone gathered round. Some noises came from behind the building and in a very short time we were picking chicken bones. This was gratis courtesy of our fellow passengers, handed to us without a word spoken. A large hubbly-bubbly was then brought out and passed round in the stillness of the warm starry desert night.

We had to change buses at Kandahar and reality now hit Rob and I in the face. There was enough money for the fare to Herat—none over for food. We could try hitching. This is not good hitching country. We decided to tighten (if that was possible) our belts. Having travelled overnight the next day was a long one, the seriousness of our situation striking home as we went without food.

I was becoming ravenous and thirsty. In the heat of the afternoon a stop was made in a small village and we went inside a domed chai-shop which was blissfully cool inside. No chai though. An unpleasant thrill rose up inside me. Thousands of miles from home and not able to buy a cup of tea—hmm. On the way out I took a slight detour and foolishly gave in to my pangs by lying down and drinking from a stream. There were some undesirable objects floating past on the surface.

As I made my way back to the bus I realised the sewer from the street ran into the stream higher up and in particular noticed that a butcher's had been disposing its waste. I tried not to think about it. It was about this time my troubles increased. At sunset the bus stopped by the roadside and as we were the only two foreigners everyone else on board got off to pay their respects to Mecca. Towards the end of a trying night we pulled into Herat.

We were now completely thrown on our own resources. This in plain English meant scrounging, begging and scavenging—survival. There was nothing for it but to stick our thumbs out. To our welcome surprise we got lift after lift from a variety of benefactors, even a local bus waived the fare. In this manner we crossed the Afghan / Iran border and reached Mashad in a day. We walked to the outskirts of the town to bivouac for the night. We had done well for food that day, many people sharing with us. There was a wild, carefree exhilaration in this mode of existence. I had probably never been so desperate and happy both at the same time. We literally had nothing to lose and had given up any notions of responsibility.

After a good night's sleep in a sand-gully we rose early. I felt refreshed. Having abandoned ourselves to the hands of fate I felt as if we could walk on water, even if we did eventually sink. Some of this was probably induced by overexposure to the sun, the run of good luck and temporary euphoria due to lack of proper food. The feeling was real enough though. This day was a Sunday and a notion came to me that was at first slightly disorientating.

Sunday is a normal day here, Friday being a rest day. The two of us had walked about a mile and were standing with not a vehicle in sight. In England there would be traditional roast dinner, I could picture it in my mind's eye. Here Rob and I were with nothing before us but barren desert stretching away as far as the eye could see, utterly penniless, with no prospects, knowing no-one and finding the language problematic. I realised how dependent the mind is on familiar cultural associations and certainties. We must have been in this spot ages and normally I would have got frustrated and panicky but time seemed to take on a different aspect. Melted into vapour. Then out of the blue comes a truck, picks us up and we're on our way.

This lift took us a good way. We sat in the front cab with the driver who was a local. He hardly spoke but occasionally passed a cheerful smile. Having had other things on my mind I had not thought of my health situation for a long while but now the simple lack of food caused internal gnawing pains to concentrate my thoughts somewhat. These would come and go as presumably my stomach was contracting.

At this stage of the journey we often passed groups of nomadic Bedouins, the trains of camels moving slowly along or saw the dark form of their large tents set up against the desert background. They became fewer and farther between as the number of villages began to increase, the Elburz Mountains appeared to the north and we neared Tehran.

We arrived late at night in the city centre—destitute. The best thing to do was move away from the busy main streets and bright lights to find a quiet place to rest. As with all cities the backstreets are only a stone's throw away. We found a dark back alley with one or two vehicles parked. The night was turning cold and apart form huddling up in a corner some overhead shelter was needed. By this time we figured that most people would be in bed so we would risk crawling underneath a car.

This we did and were soon fast asleep. It was not to last long though as I was woken up by a weird sensation of thick liquid dripping on my face. This was oil from the engine. In what had to be regarded as a bizarre arrangement, necessity once more proving to be the mother of invention, we got hold of what looked like two metal rubbish-bins, took the lids off and emptied all the waste against a side wall. We then laid up to our waists underneath the rear of the car with the rest of us inside the dustbins. In this unconventional manner we slept like logs.

A rude awakening was had in the morning by the noise and vibration of the engine starting up. The driver hadn't seen us and we scrambled out to greet a new day. Our next move was to locate the Amir Kamir, the main travellers hotel in Tehran, to see if there were any lifts going. I had stayed here before and we found it without too much difficulty. There is a first floor foyer-cum-common-room on the lines of the one in Peshawar.

Having scanned the notice-board we found just what we were looking for. Most trips required pro rata payment but free lifts were on offer and there was one with two places to Istanbul the next day. Having made the appropriate contact to secure these places we settled ourselves on the far side of the room in low easy chairs and relaxed. We had a large window behind us which let in streams of sunlight, warming our backs after the cold night on the hard ground. It was pleasant just to lounge, taking in the general comings and goings and then having a cat nap.

When I was awake again I found I had a splitting headache. Not only this but when I got up to go for a wash I could hardly stand for feeling weak and had to sit down again. The lack of food was really beginning to tell. At his stage we struck up conversation with an Oz guy sitting next to us called Zach who it turned out was going on the same trip as us. We must have looked a real state by now so as he had just got a big plate of egg salad with nan bread he hardly touched it and whilst turning his head slightly the other way pushed it towards us. We devoured it voraciously. Without it at that stage I really felt as If I would have passed out. It was a lifeline.

We exchanged tales with Zach. Having recounted our side he explained that he was going to Europe for the first time. He was our age and had been running a sheep farm for this mother for the past couple of years. He had wanted to see something of the outside world and was making the trip overland. He was deeply tanned and stocky. With his goaty beard I could picture him on a large sheep farm.

We decided that we would stick together for a little while. He may have thought we could use a little looking after. It was good to have extra company though and hear things from a different point of view. He was into music the same as we both were. Chatting away in this manner we passed the rest of the day. He had a room and as we were due out the next day we were allowed to stay in chairs. We agreed to meet up in the morning.

Morning came and the hours dragged. A bloke from Hemel Hempstead in England going the other way to us was agitated about something. I became dazy. At last late afternoon departure. The bus was virtually outside the hotel. All the passengers were Westerners which was an unfamiliar experience. The wide main streets were packed with traffic and it was hot. Curtains were essential on sunnyside windows. For what seemed like miles we crawled at snail's pace through the unvarying city. Music played on a cassette which was a tonic. Eventually the suburbs were reached, speed increased, with it there was a breeze and everyone seemed to breathe a sigh of relief. Zach handed Rob and I a bag of fruit.

Near the outskirts we saw a very smart looking set of railway passenger carriages, completely empty and stationary. With the oil here road transport is favourite but I thought it a waste the train standing there as we had been sitting around so long. However, we were now entering open country and heading out into the night. The combination of inertia and hunger kept me awake while most people dozed, one or two sleeping in the aisle. The residential areas past through were well lit and the road was smooth. One or two places looked definitely oil-influenced—like a town around a chemical plant.

I began to fantasize about food; all the popular dishes and individual items. Beer and runner beans were a recurring favourite. The vividness of what amounted to near hallucinogenic proportions was nearly as good as the real thing in that it was in fact psychologically satisfying. In this way I feasted at length without eating a morsel. With my eyes feeling like organ stops, in the early hours of the morning I dozed off.

'Alice in Wonderland' had nothing on it. I wasn't falling down or into a hole—a small hole had been born inside me, was expanding and I was becoming that hole. Or so it seemed. The miles rolled by in clear bright sunshine. Landscape became rugged, rivers sparkled through clumps of poplars shimmering in the breeze. We slowed down and were forced to come to a halt in a small town where a large crowd had gathered. There appeared to be an air of expectancy.

A central space was made by the people moving back as if jostling for position to view an imminent event. A semi-circle had been formed around the side of a low mud building the wall of which was kept clear. To the side of this a muscular bare chested figure with a shaven head appeared and made his way to the centre of the arena. A waist-high wooden block was brought forward by two men.

Then a mournful-looking individual was led out, with his arms bound together in front of him with cord, by two other men followed by what looked like a presiding official. The crowd became still. All the men in the centre withdrew bar two. A few words were spoken by the official. The forlorn figure with head bowed standing sideways to the wall put his hands on the block. There was a hush. The shaven headed man held a cleaver at his side which he raised high into the air with both hands and down it came. Blood spurted forth, two men dashed forward to bandage the figure, who had collapsed, and stemmed the flow of blood. He was then led away as the crowd quietly dispersed.

All over. Justice had been seen to be done. A robber who would rob no more. In a minute or so we were on the move. I had been about twenty yards away window side of the event. There are no prisons in this part of the world.

During the rest of the day my food dreams of the previous night recurred, haunting me like a ghost. I am being transmogrified. This part of the journey begins to dissolve into a hazy blur into which I fade in and out. The daytime heat starts to ease and we stop in the Iranian border-town of Tabriz. Having managed to scrounge some cash I whistle off to a local bakery. It is a joint full of Eastern promise. Freshly made on the premises, sweet smelling confectionery of various shapes, textures, colours and sizes are displayed in the window and in glass cabinets inside. It is all very good value and I purchase as wide a selection as possible.

Making haste back to the bus which nearly leaves without me—that would be all I need. On board the goodies are shared out all around. I devour too much too quickly but enjoy it all the same. It will have to keep me going for sometime.

Driving through the night the next day is overcast and grey with a consequent drop in temperature. This was something quite novel to me having been used to virtually permanent blue skies. It is like watching a black and white film after being used to Technicolor. The brown shades of buildings, tracks and hills reveal themselves in more depth and somehow feel more homely and enclosed, lessening the sense of vastness that exists under endless cerulean heavens.

We came to the large town of Ezrum and spot another empty stationary train. After all the constant bumping and swerving the thought of a nice steady rhythmic train journey takes on blissful proportions. Road travel in these parts is akin to some kind of fun-fair ride minus the humour devised by a malicious sadist with prolonged torture in mind. This is not exaggerating. It is small wonder I have lost considerable weight. The mobile skeleton.

At this point a few people disembarked. Zach gave us a nudge. Sometime ago he had pointed out a guy to us a few seats away. He had straight long blond hair down his back to below his waist, a beard of equal length and had sat rigid bolt upright with his bright blue eyes staring straight ahead of himself without ever uttering a word or even seeming to be on this planet.

"He's on a trip of his own," was Zach's comment.

Rob and I had grinned. There was a likeable down-to-earth characteristic about Zach, which he expressed in short, to the point phrases. As if a start button in his back had been pushed this previously inert figure now methodically got up, loaded his rucksack on, made his way down the aisle and got off the bus, never to be seen again.

We were informed later by his previous immediate neighbour that words had passed his lips as that on enquiry he said that he was changing at Ezrum to make his way south and then westwards to the coast at Izmir which is a place of classical antiquity. Perhaps he was going to catch one of the phantom trains that never move, as there is a line, at least on a map, in that direction.

Once more into the breach. I begin to feel this ride is either going to make a man of me or be the end of me. Hope is on the former, smart money, the latter. About two days to Istanbul. I'm getting in such a condition I don't take in my surroundings anymore, sleeping erratically for short periods. The weather stays cloudy and mild as the gradual proliferation of hillside chalet style houses tells us that we are on the far outskirts of eastern Istanbul.

This is during the middle of the day and for a few miles we are joined by a stretch of mythical railway track running parallel to the road, come back to taunt us. Perfectly good track and not a train in sight, not even near the city—weird. As the topography evens out the stacks of hillside houses give way to blocks of flats with youths playing football in the open spaces. Rurality has given way to Suburbia. In the late afternoon, having crossed the Bosphorus I am back in Europe. The bus rolls up in front of the Pudding Shop.

As people started to get off the bus Rob and I rose to make our own exit. At this point we were splitting up with Zach who was heading off somewhere on his own. We said our goodbyes and as Rob and I climbed down the bus steps Zach called out good luck.

A streetwise looking fellow passenger who was already standing on the pavement looked at us with a grin and said "You look like you'll need it."

I had felt temporarily elated when we had finally arrived in Istanbul sore and travel-weary. Now we were standing at the roadside, with the passing comment just made to us, I realised just what a bad state I was in. After so much bodily inertia and lack of circulation I could hardly move through stiffness. It was as if I had shrunk.

We had already decided to check into the Pudding Shop (another popular caravanserai) and worry about payment later as we were at present not fit to try going on. We spoke to the receptionist, giving him a hard luck story. He must have taken pity on us as we were allowed a bunk-bed in the top-storey dormitory. As we passed through the usual communal gathering area we attracted several looks. Amongst the varied and motley crew this takes some doing. Truly we must have presented a woeful bedraggled picture.

It was when we came to climb the stairs I realised I could not make it. I was too weak. With a great final effort, one arm on Rob's shoulder the other on the inner stair-rail I managed to haul up the three flights. There we found a spare bunk and collapsed, dead to the world.

We came to in late evening and Rob suggested going downstairs to get the lay of the land. At first I agreed but on trying to get up didn't have the strength so he went on his own. I lay and rested. When he returned there was not much to report so we called it a night.

In the morning it was obvious that we weren't going to be able to carry on with our plan to try hitching through Europe so we agreed to go to the British Consulate was the most sapient course to take. I had benefited from the night's sleep and was able to go downstairs unaided. Explaining to the manager what our intentions were he was helpful and informed us the Consulate was located in the modern quarter of the city a long distance from where we were in the old part. Therefore he advised us to take a taxi there. On telling him we had absolutely no money he said he would speak to the driver and arrange things. For this we were most grateful.

A telephone call was made and our transport duly arrived. From rags to riches. Hardly, but it felt that way as we cruised off, chauffeur driven, through the uneven, winding streets that slope steeply down and then abrubtly rise again. This area is like a honeycomb and is fascinating to move through. Driving over the Galata bridge, which crosses the Golden Horn, an inlet of the Bosphorus, we entered the European suburbs. The architecture and layout could well be that of another city the contrast is so great.

At length we reached our destination. The Consulate is a grand impressive building making us feel insignificant and out of place especially given our appearance which would make an amazing contrast to the dignitaries that must come here. However, we were British citizens and this was a piece of British territory.

We made enquiries and stated our business. As we had no appointment it was necessary to wait. We were motioned across an inner courtyard. After the bustle of the outside world there was a civilised sense of stilll order as we crossed the cool,wide paved space dipped in shadow, lined with tomb-like dark windows and only the gentle splashing sound of the water-jet from a small ornamental fountain, which was set symetrically central to the outer walls, playing and echoing. Feeling like insects we opened and passed through a pair of tall doors, half-paned rich sandy wooden with large shining octagonal brass knobs which you could barely grasp in your hand to turn. It was no less imposing inside.

A quietly spoken official showed us where to wait and then withdrew. We sat on some bottle-green leathered straight high-backed chairs which were lined with studding that stood out from the deep brown of the wood. Here we were left alone in a high stucco-ceilinged room, with chequer-board stoned flooring, marble columns and large fan-shaped palm-plants for decoration. We waited in a silence in which you could hear a pin drop. And wait we did. Eventually the official reappeared and ushered us through into a further recess of the inner sanctum. Here we explained our situation and how we came to be in it. This was received with obvious frowning displeasure and hardly conceiled annoyance.

However, arrangements were made for our repatriation. We had to surrender our passports which we could collect on our final departure. In the meantime we gave the name of where we were staying and it was organised so that we could have a daily expense allowance through the reception there until our tickets came. When it transpired we had taken a taxi coming here we were curtly informed that there was such a thing as public transport.

The whole thing should take a few days. Feeling like errant schoolboys being dismissed from the headmaster's study we left the building, inwardly greatly relieved. On our way out we went to a section where we were given receipts for the passports and our first day's expenses. It was the first time we had held money for ages. This did not go to our heads as we decided to walk back to the hotel.

We made our way, mostly downhill, back to the Galata bridge. This is a long wide bridge. About halfway across, as fate will always have it, I received a severe attack of 'Delhi belly'. In the very little warning that one receives I made a frantic dash for the other side. But it was a token gesture. To use a mockingly appropriate pun, I was literallygoing through the motions. Having first been seized by panic with nowhere to hide, believing yourself to be the focus of attention, you realise that not a single person is looking at you and you might as well be invisible as everyone hurries by. This is superceded by more tangible feelings closer to home. I was still wearing my baggy lime-green pyjama trousers, cheesecloth top and plimsolls. The trousers were now not so lime-green or baggy.

With the panic over a sense of almost forlorn depression immediately set in. It was strange after everything I had been through but at that moment I stood still in the middle of that bridge, a grown man, and could nearly have cried. I suspect it was release of tension. This passed in a moment though as I shrugged my shoulders and thought to myself, what the hell—it's only nature, and strolled merrily on my way without a care in the world—I do believe I began to whistle.

Rob caught up with me and asked what I was doing. When we got to the other side there was an aquarium he wanted to visit as he had a tank of tropical fish at home. I was not into this which annoyed him somewhat. I agreed to wait for him outside. While he did this I went down along the nearby quayside where many vessels were harboured.

There was a fresh catch of fish from the morning and at small cost you could buy some cooked on a brazier standing on the walkway. There is nothing like the smell of this combined with the sea air and the general waterside atmosphere. Despite my immediately recent experience I succumbed, placating my conscience by figuring that it would be fat-free and high in protein. I sat down by the edge with my purchase and watched the boats plying their way through the choppy water.

Meeting up with Rob we made our way back. My pyjamas and I were clearly going to have to part company. They were beyond saving and I felt sad about this as I thought them brilliant trousers. There was no doubt about it though, so shortly they were dumped in a bin. The question was, what else? Rob was of a smaller stature than myself but I had lost so much weight that I could squeeze into his spare pair of filthy jeans. This he kindly let me do.

There was a well known dry-cleaner's nearby to which I paid a visit. The girl running the joint was American and clearly amused at my plight. I told her my predicament. She laughingly agreed to have the jeans cleaned straightaway while I waited in the shop, top stretched down, hands folded in front. I wasn't going anywhere. Unfortunately the jeans shrunk a bit so it was a further squeeze getting back into them, but I made it. It was a bit like shedding my Eastern skin and working my way back into my Western one.

After resting up for a while, in the evening we thought to try a small eating-shop we had seen close by used by locals. It was a short walk and it was pleasant to take in the night air, then sit and listen to the local chatter over a cup of tea in the small crowded café that was warmly lit with hanging oil-lamps. There was an intimacy about the place and the home-made soup with chunks of white bread and lemon sections that you could squeeze into it was delicious. It was clear vegetable as I was trying to avoid fat and also get an intake of viatmins. At this point I felt as if I were coming under a heavy influenza.

During the night my temperature rose and I perspired profusely. I got little sleep, tossing and turning and then started to shiver. I slept in the end but awoke to feeling numb and virtually rigid. I hoped this would ease but it did not so I decided I would not venture forth that day but stay in bed. Rob went out and the people in the dorm came and went. There was no real window with a view in here so I just lay there staring at the ceiling, as I had the upper bunk, hoping to recuperate. Instead of this I seemed to get worse but by the time Rob came back I felt duty bound to make an effort to visit the café of the previous evening for some nourishment. Rob commented on my lack of conversation. I found it physically difficult to talk and could only just swallow the soup. We left early and I had another bad night.

Apart from feeling physically ill this was getting to me psychologically. True to character I entered on more folly. As I had passed through the bar area downstairs I had noticed brightly coloured bottles of what I took to be wine on display. This turned out to be the case. Local wine and cheap. I obtainted a bright cerise-pink one which I went back upstairs with. I only took two or three swallows and was taken with a violent urge to vomit. My weakness, together with the hidden potency of the wine that I had not allowed for combined to strike me. As I was going for the washroom which was near the stairs the world started to spin around me. I grabbed out for something to hold onto but the outside stair wall which was spiral at this point had no hand rail. In consequence I fell, having lost control, tumbling down several flights. The next thing I was vaguely aware of was being carried by several people back up and then blank again.

I came to a few hours later. On going to rise I found I was too dizzy and feeble to do so. Laying back in some distress I found this unnerving. For the first time I was afraid. There was nothing to do but be still. Time dragged and although I was in no pain as such I was taken by an incipient sickly feeling which seemed to hang over me. It was late afternoon judging by the fading light when Rob came in and asked me how I was feeling. He had brought a bag of tangerines in for me. Obviously I would not be going out that night so he went off alone.

I was no better next day. I hadn't been able to swallow and periodically brought up flem. I grabbed what looked like a white flannel hanging on the bunk next to me to wipe with. Later on a fellow came in and put this on his balding head. Despite my state I nearly died (humourwise). He was extremely irrate and it was all I could do to keep a straight face, feigning innocence and denying any knowledge of what turned out to be his sun-hat.

Rob brought more fruit in and said there was still no news from the Consulate. By the next day I was getting serious and thankfully on phoning we were told that our tickets were ready. A taxi took us to collect them and our passports. It was a strain being out again but everything was sorted out and we went back directly to the rail station. The train was due to leave in two hours time. The first train since Pakistan. It was in the platform and we were able to board, having a compartment to ourselves. I felt very fragile. After seclusion the world appeared dreamlike.

Dusk began to fall and everywhere in the city lights twinkled into life. In a bright yellow glare station-porters began to bring luggage along the platform, newspaper and confectionery hawkers were trying to sell their wares. Departure would not be long. Right on time we moved out of the station. The destination was Paris, due to take three days. We still had the compartment to ourselves so we stretched out and went to sleep.

After a long night's rest we awoke to find ourselves trundling through southern Europe. Rob went in search of tea from the buffet car. We were joined temporarily by other passengers at various times during the day as the occasional stops were made. By late evening we were unaccompanied again which was a blessing in terms of sleeping arrangements. The next morning I awoke feeling very strange indeed. A feeling hard to describe, otherworldly. I was able to sit up all right.

Rob was already up and was staring at me. "Take a look in the mirror," he said.

There was one placed over the head of the seating. I received one of the weirdest shocks I'd ever had. It wasn't me. Only it was me and the whites of my eyes were completely bright-yellow. My complexion was a paler shade of the same colour. It was disorientating and I looked again in disbelief. It was as if I had been alienated from myself. I sat back-down in a state of mild shock. “You’d better see a doctor as soon as you get back,” quoth Rob.

That day the compartment filled right up as we travelled through Italy and went weaving our way through Alpine scenery; tunnels, mountains and long sweeping wooded valleys. As night came on we were entering the last leg of the journey. My condition hadn’t improved and my eyes felt like organ stops pulled fully out.

We had to sit upright during the night which didn’t help sleep but in the first grey light of dawn we entered Paris. Here we had to change to go on to Calais. We got on board an early ferry and I was called to the bar. Here I supped a pint of beer. The first few sips were heavenly and the rest went down quickly but this was followed by nausea. I sat the rest of the crossing out with Rob, feeling dreadful.

We didn’t have long for a rail connection at Dover and were soon on our way rolling through the Kent countryside. Rob and I hadn’t spoken recently, no doubt because we had been so much in each other’s company. He asked me if I was trying to catch some flies. I became aware that I had been sitting rather gormlessly with my mouth wide open. I was slightly irritated at Rob but realised he had a point. We had been through a lot together and I don’t think it had really dawned on us that we would very soon be parting company. One of the things he wanted to do when he got back was go to the Bingley Hall where he had seen a lot of big name rock bands. As the train slowed into London he advised me again to see a doctor at the earliest opportunity. We pulled into Victoria and came to a halt. Collecting our gear off the luggage-rack we disembarked.

We walked down the platform together without speaking and through the ticket-barrier. He was getting the tube and I was catching a coach. This was the moment of parting. We wished each other luck and after a quick mutual look turned on our separate ways. We had not even exchanged addresses. It felt strange to be solitary again. I was soon among the crowd as I had to walk several hundred yards to the coach terminus.

My timing was good again. A coach in an hour. I took this opportunity to avail myself of the sanitary facilities where I received another shock. My liquid was orange. I knew I was in trouble. I began to sense a chill and felt unearthly. My coach took me to Chelmsford where I was to take a local bus. I had five minutes to spare so I made a call from a phone box to announce my imminent arrival.

Then I was on a double-decker for the last section. It was all quite unreal. The bus pulled into Braintree where I was met. At first I was unrecognised so I had to verbally announce myself. I didn't say much. An hour later I was sat at table in Gosfield eating a meal, which went down quickly but unfortunately went through me. I had weighed fourteen stone when I left. I was now seven. I went to bed, glad to have made it but knowing I was in a bad way.

III. ENTER THE RAKE

I SLEPT WELL THAT NIGHT. It was good to sleep in a bed again. It was also nice to wake up in familiar surroundings. I didn't do much that day but just take it easy, drink some tea and clean up. The jeans I had been wearing could stand up on their own. My top had become a second skin. In fact it took a few washes to discover the real me. If shoes could talk those plimsolls could tell a tale. I was on my own during the day and it was quiet but because of my gastric situation I knew I ought to go to Braintree the next day to see the doctor.

I underwent a thorough check-up and was given some pills with no precise diagnosis. By the following day I had deteriorated even further and stayed in bed. During the middle of the day I developed a terrible itching sensation which caused me to scratch. When I did so the area swelled up into large welts which formed a hard yellow mass. This began to spread. It became located in all the crevices: between the toes, behind the knees, in front of the elbows, between the legs, underneath the arms and behind the ears. I tried to stop scratching as I realised that wherever I did so a growth would appear, but couldn't and they started to join up, a hard inflexible covering so I could hardly move. It was painful and burning.

Then most frighteningly the swelling formed over my eyes and mouth virtually sealing them up. I began to scream with fear. My body was covered from head to foot in one great lump. Fortunately I was found in this condition and the doctor was called. I managed to swallow two tablets and the doctor came out. He took one look at me and called an ambulance. In the dark of early evening I was taken to hospital and into intensive care where I was sedated.

The next thing I was aware of was being surrounded by specialists and nurses all wearing face-masks standing outside an isolation tent that covered my bed, inside a sealed unit. At this stage I learned that I may possibly have a dangerous form of hepatitis. It was morning and the day passed without me knowing much about it. Nobody was permitted into the room without wearing a mask and I was under sedation.

The following day I appeared to have stabilised. Apparently it had been a close call and I was lucky to be there. Something inside me had held on. I realised that the swelling had gone down and I became more aware of my surroundings. It really was like waking from a nightmare. I was still very weak but the intense nausea had vanished and I had a sense of release.

I was only able to take a little soup but it tasted good and I was satisfied. My insides were still in turmoil though, causing problems. By the end of the day I had visitors and felt as if I had made a step back into the world. Over the next few days I made a slow but steady recovery and gradually regained my appetite. I was on a fat-free diet and was examined by various specialists. Eventually I was allowed to get up and put a dressing-gown on.

I began to regain my strength and even put on a bit of weight. By the seventh day the yellowness from my eyes and skin had disappeared and I was allowed to walk on the ward. This was a big event for me to be able to talk to other patients and use the lounge area at the bottom of the ward. It was wonderful to be back amongst people after the isolation. I still stayed in there however as I hadn't been fully cleared. All sorts of tests were performed on me. It seemed I was some sort of medical curiosity. At last, after thirteen days—lucky for some—I was told I could leave next day.

A consultant came in to see me in the morning and said that I was to stay on a fat-free diet and abstain from alcohol at least until my out-patients appointment which was for a fortnight's time. There were further tests required as it appeared no conclusive diagnosis had as yet been formed. When the time came to leave the outside felt like a new, fresh place.

Back home again I still had to take it easy after being so incapacitated and found I slept a lot. It was good to be wearing ordinary clothes again, drink coffee whenever I felt like it and play music. After a while I took a walk outside and thoroughly enjoyed it. It was fantastic to be alive.

I had to go back to the hospital three times in all but it never was completely found out what was wrong with me and would ever remain a mystery. As the weeks passed I began to lead a normal life again. I started working and playing sport. Socialising was enjoyable and I found I could drink in moderation although I should never consume spirits again and still avoided over-fatty foods. My body told me how far to go. It was a condition that would always be with me, lying dormant, but by using common sense I should be all right. I had youth on my side.

Come the summer I started to do some local travelling and began to get itchy feet again. I decided to get a Euro rail card which you could obtain for a reasonable amount and gave you unlimited travel throughout the rail network in Europe for a certain period. By catching a lot of overnighters I could maximise my travelling and the amount of places I could see. It also minimised my expenditure.

It was fun and had a great sense of adventure waking up to a completely new place in the morning. I had crossed the Channel in daylight spending my time on the ferry on deck, mostly at the rear, leaning over watching the swell and trail of the ship as the coastline receded. The rest of the way I sat next to a very fine slide-guitarist. I had no plan in mind. I just caught any train whose destination appealed and was leaving soon.

From Paris, where I bought a huge lump of cheese which I lived on for three days, I found myself in the south of France, Italy and Switzerland again. After I had used my ticket up I arranged to do some grape-picking in the Beaujolais region. This included meals, which were enormous and accommodation, which was comfortable.

There was a constant supply of wine on tap—too much—and I brushed up my spoken French although I found the language harder to understand here than in Zurich. At the end of working sixteen days straight from dawn to dusk I received a big lump sum cash in hand and went walking down the road a happy man.

The lanes round here were quiet and pleasant to stroll along. You'd think I'd had enough but I picked a bunch of grapes from the side of the road. They are black thick clustered bunches.

As I came into a small village a lady was airing out bedding from a first floor window of a house and called out "bonjour". I replied ditto. One of those times when you really mean the words you say. Some elderly gentlemen were seated outside a café with glasses of wine. They sky was full-blue and the late October sun shone down warmly. The world was my oyster.

I had a mind to go through Spain and down to Morocco but wasn't absolutely fixed on it. I got a branch train from Ville Franche into Lyon and then went down to Avignon which I thought I'd explore for a bit. The train I happened to get from there took me along the Riviera and I ended up walking round Nice all night. I got fed up with loud discos so went down to the palm-lined beach and lay down for a while. The Mediterranean flopped on the shingle. I made an early morning raid on a patisserie and then boarded the first train out, passing Monte Carlo and ending up in Genoa, travelling through some exotic scenery.

I needed to retrace my steps if I was going to Africa so did so. After making a detour to visit Turin I headed for Marseilles passing back through San Remo, Antibes, Cannes and Toulon. I must have made an error at Marseilles. Thinking I was catching an overnighter to Madrid, having stopped at Arles I knew something was wrong when going through Tolouse in the middle of the night instead of heading down the coast to Barcelona. I woke up next morning in Bordeaux.

There was a train to Paris leaving soon, so on instinct I caught it, first buying a bottle of good claret at bargain price. Unbelievably, in just over a week I had got through nearly all my dough.

When I got to Paris I was actually going to head for the Embassy but as I was making my way there along a wide pavement, staring gloomily at the ground what should catch my eye but a banknote. Equivalent—it turned out—to exactly what I needed for my fare. My gloom turned to a smile. I even had enough for a beer on the ferry. I decided I was going to pack up travelling for the while and went into a hiatus.

Come early summer I was off again, this time getting a not so 'magic' bus to Athens. The legroom leaves something to be desired and stops were infrequent although a break for a couple of hours at Graz in Austria enabled me to purchase some excellent Weiner schnitzel and a superb bottled beer served to me by a beautiful and helpful lady.

A further evening break in Greece saw me downing a bottle of wine to ease the discomforture. This had all been done on the spur of the moment and after spending some time in Athens I moved on. I had considered flying but that was as far as it got. I took a ramshackle train to Salonika where I had been before.

I liked it here for some reason and stopped for a while. I had a very reasonably priced large, tastefully furnished room in a quiet hotel with a big courtyard garden awash with plants and pots. The dusky corridors inside seemed to echo of the past. There is a long waterfront here which I enjoyed strolling along.

Out of the blue one evening the walls in my room began to shake, plaster cracking and the whole fabric vibrated. This lasted about a minute as a guess. It was an earthquake. It had been worse in other parts of the city as the devastation outside revealed when I ventured forth next day—time to move on I thought. I went to the rail station which was like a huge sports stadium with a vast shiny tiled concourse—the most impressive building in the city. It was crowded with many people carrying their belongings whose homes had been affected by the quake. Presumably a lot of them were going to relatives in the country. It was awful to see them in their distressed state and only later on did I find out how widespread the devastation had been.

I bought a single to Munich. On entering Germany I was asked to produce my passport by two large armed police with dogs. I didn't refuse them. My idiosyncratic modus operandi resulted on this occasion in me landing up in Munich at midnight with no more departures that night. A hotel was out of the question (usual lack of funds) and a heavy police presence meant the station was too. But hey, look on the bright side, an unexpected lengthly solo pedestrian tour of the deserted streets of Munich.

In truth it is one of the best ways to see a place. By about two everywhere apart from one or two night-clubs was shut up and the wide streets were empty. I was impressed by the cleanliness and ended up enjoying taking in the varied architecture. It was all well lit and during the day with all the bustle you could never get a view of a city like this. It was four o' clock before I knew it so I made my way back to the station which reopened at five.

When I arrived there was still some time before it opened so I sat down on the steps outside and waited. It was just daylight by now and as I sat there a peculiar occurrence took place. I spotted a figure coming lurching along the middle of the road. It was a man and he was all over the place. I thought it was early in the morning to be in that state, but perhaps he'd been to an all-nighter. Slightly disconcertingly as he came level with the steps to the station entrance he paused, turned and started to stagger up them. I thought he was going to approach me.

As he came nearer I realised he was covered in blood. He had a great wound on his forehead and the blood was streaming down his face and splattered all over the front of his clothes. His coat was badly torn and covered with large dirt marks. He didn't seem to be aware of my existence at all and made his way to the station doors. On finding they were locked he turned back down the steps and went on his way, staggering into the distance.

Apart from surprise one of the first things I thought of was to see if he needed help but it all happened so quickly out of the blue and he was in such a world of his own that before I knew it he was gone. It did strike me that he may have been in a road accident and be concussed or trouble of some other sort. However the street was now empty and the bloody phantom of Munich had vaporized. A strange start to the day.

The doors were opened and in I went with a few others that had arrived. I went to check out the information-board and then make ticket enquiries. When I went to purchase a ticket I realised I hadn't got enough marks on me so went to the

Bureau de Change. This didn't open till eight so I still had some time to kill. I found a seat on the main concourse and watched as the station came to life. One by one the early trains started to arrive. These were workers' trains which although it was still only five-thirty were packed and people came pouring off them, dispersing to various parts of the station.

As I sat there activity began behind me and the waiting-rooms and kiosks were opened. This included what I realised was a large beerhouse. As the doors were opened huge wooden barrels were rolled out onto the waiting area and then stood upright—one of them close to me. I wondered at this.

My perplexity was soon cleared as with the arrival of another train several huge well-dressed men came purposefully towards the barrels and then stood by them. Within seconds a Fräulein in traditional folk-dress came out carrying great thick litre glass mugs of brau, golden and foaming, which she placed on top of the barrel near me. She had platted blonde hair, a skirt with straps, white socksthe lot. It was out of a fairy-tale. No sooner was this done than the men raised the handles and downed these litres in one go. I couldn't believe it.

The Fräulein returned with duplicates and large filled bread rolls which were consumed with the second drink, which wasn't drunk so quickly as the first (although there wasn't much in it) but to complete my confoundment, a third was! They then slapped some money down on the barrel tops and were gone. The Fräulein cleared the top and took the money. It was all over in a couple of minutes in a most efficient business-like way. What a way to go to work I thought! The place was buzzing for about an hour or so, then a calmer air pervaded although no less busy.

When I went to change my currency I found that I hadn't quite enough fare for the route via Paris. The girl at the Bureau was very helpful. At her suggestion and with the aid of some financial jiggery-pokery she worked out for me enough for the fare via Brussels and some over. I got myself a coffee and awaited the ten o' clock departure. The station had cleared by this time and I boarded my train in relaxed fashion. It was a clear sunny day as the train rolled through Bavaria.

I was glad that I was going on this particular route as not long after Stuttgart the line followed the banks of the Rhine for a long time, passing through some splendid castled scenery, hugging the wide river for some stretches, with enormous cargo barges looking like the heads of great under-water sea-monsters, as it weaved and curved its way along towards the North Sea. Passing Mann-heim and Mainz where the river is joined by the Main and is swollen again at Koblenz by the Moselle amid high terraced vineyards like a patchwork quilt draped on the landscape. On reaching Cologne my route parted from the river and headed west for Belgium. I passed through the conservative feeling city of Brussels and onto Ostend.

For the next few summer months I worked on a building site, building my own strength up, play-ing sport, devouring three meals a day and consuming vast quantities of beer. I was saving a fair bit with the idea of flying somewhere. I thought of Jamaica but the cost was surprisingly high so in the end I got a ticket for Delhi.

AGAIN

I WAS IN GOOD CONDITION when I set off and as usual travelled light. All I had was my passport, traveller's cheques, a music paper and the clothes I stood up in. I think the airport officials thought it a bit odd I had no luggage, it meant though that I was first on the plane and had pick of the seats. Naturally I chose a window with a good view. The plane gradually filled up. I had not flown before but was curious rather than nervous. When take-off came it seemed the earth had dropped out from underneath me and England became a chequered pattern far away.

The first stop was Damascus which was lit-up at night and then Abu Dhabi during the day. When the doors were opened here it was like opening an oven door—I stayed inside. I was seated with an Indian family who were going to stay with relatives. They didn't care for the food that was regularly brought round so I ate theirs as well as my own—might as well stock up. I didn't sleep much during the flight and it was strange to think, when touching down in Delhi, that what had taken me so long before had this time only been a matter of hours.

The customs people here were even more suprised at my mode of travel, but I just breezed out of the airport and hopped into a three-wheeler taxi. The first thing that struck me again was all the monkeys roaming about. I asked for a hotel area and sat back.

I was taken to the old part of Delhi where the streets are very narrow. It has a very dodgy feel and I didn't intend to stay long. I had a dreadful drink of I don't know what and a restless night, exacerbated by jet-lag no doubt. The next morning I was up early and off. I made my way to Connaught Circus which is a gathering area. I saw an offer of a flight to Khatmandu which was tempting, but didn't go for it. Instead I went for the old favourite.

A taxi took me bumping passed the Red Fort and onwards. As we did so, giant wayside posterboards urging birth control were to be seen. The heaps of rubbish at the side of the road are something, and at one point the rotting carcass of a horse had to be negotiated. We arrived at the train temple for central and eastern India. I decided to travel first-class. At small cost I had a whole spacious compartment to myself, replete with easy chair, table, washing facilities, the lot.

Guided by the wind I found myself heading for Benares (modern Varanasi)—trainwise. This place is really packed. I got a pedal rickshaw for the first and only time. I seemed to have a rapport with my guide who, for an agreed sum, took me all over.

To be anything other than lost here would be impossible. I went to the river, the Ganges, and went in, then went to a chai-shop. Two months here was all I felt the need for and was on the move again passing back through Delhi. There was a warm monsoon downpour when I stopped over that looked like it was set in. I made my way on to Pakistan and Lahore.

On my way I met up with a New Zealander who was in India to follow the England cricket tour and was exploring the country before it started. He was staying overnight in Lahore so we passed some time together strolling about. I told him of my past experiences in the country and he suggested I should write about them sometime. During the evening we bumped into some Poles (met a group of Polish travellers) to whom we gave various directions as if we lived there. It was humid and we discovered one of the best ways to be cool for a few hours is to spend them in a cinema. There was a Hollywood film showing and it felt incongruous watching it amid an audience who clearly weren't au fait with the language or plot.

On reaching Peshawar I had to apply for a visa to Afghanistan. The office for this was some way out so I took a horse and trap. A sedate form of locomotion. I was soon to be making another journey up the Khyber and thence to Kabul. When I got there I managed by word of mouth to hear of a bungalow that was going for a peppercorn rent on the outskirts and managed to secure this. It was like a log cabin and was spacious. This I had to myself.

It had turned cold at the higher altitude necessitating warmer clothing but I was able to make a fire and have hot baths. It was also very quiet and serene. A true break from turmoil. I slept well and enjoyed cooking my own concoctions from the limited provisions I had bought. This was one of the calmest times I ever had.

True to the proverb it came to an end and I journeyed on by local transport to Herat. Here I decided to take a last breather before pushing back to Europe. It was warmer again and I spent several timeless afternoons walking along the pine avenues in the haze. When the shutter shops open in the evening they are a real delight. It was whilst looking around them one night I happened to meet a Canadian who told me of a bus leaving on the morrow for Europe. I had felt it was time to be going so plumped for this. Within twelve hours I was on my way. The passengers were all Westerners and a nice bunch of people. There were shift drivers so we didn't stop till we reached Tehran where one of our party headed south for Isfahan.

There had been some mechanical problems with the vehicle so an enforced stopover was made whilst these were attended to. It transpired that they were rectified in the nick of time for the very day we were due to leave trouble broke out in the city. It was during the morning in fact that I had just gone out to get a bit of exercise. With no warning at all there was a terrific 'rat-tat-tat' sound and instinctively I fell to the ground along with all the other pedestrians.

Temporarily frozen, I caught the sight out of the corner of one eye of a trickle, leading to a pool, of deep-crimson. When it felt all right to move I cautiously began looking around. There were people lying dead and wounded everywhere. Everything was quiet now, but it was not a peaceful quiet, rather as if held in suspended animation. I made my way hurriedly back to the hotel and in about an hour amid a great deal of confusion we made our way through thronging crowds out of the city. It would appear a revolution was taking place.

I found out later on that I had departed from Kabul at an opportune time as a matter of a day or two later tanks had rolled into the streets.

The engine trouble reoccurred at decreasing intervals and it began to look like this vehicle wasn't going to make the trip. Sure enough, in the dead of night, it finally packed up on us. Fortunately we were on the outskirts of a small town. One of the drivers went to a lodging-house with us and arranged a refund on our fares. We were not far from Turkey at this stage.

We went our separate ways in the morning and I caught local transport through to Ankara. The perennial deniro problem was raising its ugly head again. I hung around Ankara for two days in pouring rain and squelching mud in search of economical transport. There was nothing doing on the hitching front so I bit the bullet and spent my last money on a fare to Instanbul.

Twice looks like carelessness. This was déjà vu without the feeling. I knew the way this time anyhow—Consulatewise. There was a different interviewer on this occasion and his reaction was correspondingly altered. I had to admit my voice and speech felt peculiar even to me. I had spoken such a mixture of foreign and local dialects lately that my words came out a real jumble not helped by a hoarse voice. This in contrast to the plain well-spoken English of my interviewer. I do believe if it were not for my passport it would have been no go. However, in due course things were grudgingly arranged—on condition. My passport was to be stamped to the effect of my not being able to leave the U.K. again without a return ticket. I was also tersely told that this was a Consulate and not a travel agency.

On leaving I managed to obtain for the first and only time in Turkey a cup of genuine Turkish coffee. This came in a doll's house-size cup and saucer and is like black treacle. I sat at a table outside a café in the sunshine. This being the modern European sector of the city and where I was high up on a hillside there was a panoramic view of the Bosphorus, the sea of Marmara and Old Istanbul with its minorets. The coffee was like nectar.

I returned to my hotel and awaited completion of my arrangements. I was in good health and took the opportunity to explore the older parts of the city. The weather was autumnal and still, as I walked past the old wooden buildings down by the non-commercial waterside. It was a time for reflection. I meandered into a park where leaves were falling and drank a beaker of freshly squeezed orange juice obtained from a nearby vendor.

I was to travel through Bulgaria which required a visa, hence a slight delay, but was then ready to leave. It was marginally cheaper by train so that was how I was bound. Going down to the station I bought a whole roast chicken and boarded the train. This was one of the last 'Orient Express' trains to leave Istanbul. Although the rolling stock was a shadow of its former glory the route it covered was the same. I sat back and left the East behind.

I have to admit that trundling through Bulgaria was interesting although Sofia appeared on the surface a dismal place, but to be fair this impression might well have been determined to an extent by the grey weather. I perked up when I was able to get a decent cup of coffee from the refreshment car for the first time as the train pulled out of

Trieste. Arriving in Venice early morning, departure wasn't due again until late afternoon, for reasons best known to the railway, which gave me the chance to look around. The first thing I did was buy an ice-cream, which was delicious. I rested on a low wall and let the warm sun soak into my bones. Venice is of course crawling with tourists but of all the places I'd known it had a very relaxed feeling to it. It is people orientated, the lack of noise and the harmonic pace of life being due to—no wheels!

There was a cloudless deep-blue sky which reflected off the water everywhere onto the buildings. Instead of hoards of people jostling and bumping into one another they seemed to intermingle like one giant kaleidoscopic crawling snake that weaved its way through the alleys and over the bridges across the canals. It is quite easy to find a quieter part and this I unwittingly did. Before I realised it I was in a very narrow dark alley in which there seemed to be an almost audible hushed silence, when something caught my eye.

In a carved inlet in the side of a wall was a miniature statue that had a small posy of fresh flowers placed at its feet. This was like a tiny shrine. Apart form the religious connotations I found this brief moment very beautiful.

I passed several churches whose doors were open and glimpsed some wonderful architecture. I did not have time to investigate more fully but did make some time however to pay a visit to a small uncrowded restaurant where I had a huge delicious meal of pasta and sauces with good wine. It was not expensive. I seemed to drift back to the station and float out of Venice.

Passing through low flat green rice fields, Padua and Verona, next stop Milan, but not for long; time to grab a pizza, some cheese, a bag of fresh olives, a bunch of black grapes and a bottle of red wine—well why not? Some of this provenda I exchanged for a banana by facial communication with a pleasant looking man and what I took to be his young daughter. I had the strange feeling that he thought I was hungry.

The train enters the Alps by night passing through tunnels and then skirting a lake in which the moon reflects off the still water, interrupted now and then by the silhouettes of clumps of fir trees. Some places in Switzerland look like you could eat off the pavement. Luzern and Basle were passed, then Mulhouse, Strasbourg, Nancy, Metz and Reims, finally Paris.

The last leg is to Boulogne. I have a few hours to wait for a night-ferry. This is spent walking along the waterfront and then in a welcoming bistro where music is playing and I have a spaghetti Bolognese. England is entered at dawn and I arrive imperceptibly in London and onwards.